A Glaze of Color

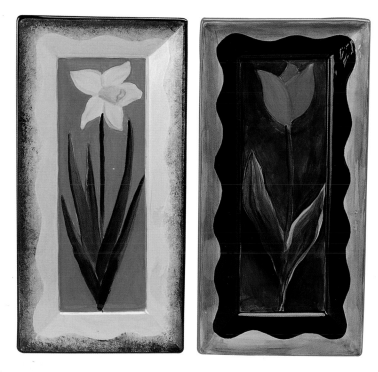

A Glaze of Color

CREATING COLOR AND DESIGN ON CERAMICS

Jane Davies

PHOTOGRAPHY BY JOHN POLAK

Watson-Guptill Publications
New York

Senior Acquisitions Editor: Joy Aquilino
Editor: Marian Appellof
Designer: Areta Buk / Thumb Print
Production Manager: Ellen Greene

Text set in Weiss

All artworks illustrated in this book are by the author, Jane Davies,
unless credited otherwise.

Kiln photographs on page 107 are courtesy of L & L Kiln Mfg. (left and
center) and Skutt Ceramic Products (right).

First published in 2004 by
Watson-Guptill Publications,
Nielsen Business Media, a division of The Nielsen Company
770 Broadway, New York, N.Y. 10003
www.watsonguptill.com

Library of Congress Control Number: 2003116521

ISBN 0-8230-2119-X

Manufactured in China

First printing, 2004

2 3 4 5 6 7 8 / 11 10 09 08 07

ACKNOWLEDGMENTS

I would like to thank my parents, Beverly
and Jim Davies, and my partner, Dean
Nimmer, for their editorial and moral
support; the artists who contributed to
this book—Janno Gay, Joan Rothchild
Hardin, Susan Kramer, Kristen Mills,
and Susan Steinberg; senior acquisitions
editor Joy Aquilino of Watson-Guptill,
for signing me on to make this book a
reality; my editor, Marian Appellof, and
my photographer, John Polak, both of
whom have been a pleasure to work
with; and Areta Buk, for her skillful book
design. Thanks also to Christopher and
Adrienne Kimball for generously lending
their house for photo shoots. Additional
thanks go to Arnold Howard of Paragon
Industries, L.P.; Stephen Lewicki of L & L
Kiln Mfg.; and Mike Sievers of Skutt
Ceramic Products, for providing information about and photographs of their kilns.

Contents

INTRODUCTION

DECORATING POTTERY is a richly rewarding medium that offers an endless variety of creative expression, whether you're a novice or an experienced artist. Besides plates, cups, and bowls for the table, you can make beautiful accessories for your home, such as lamps, vases, and decorative platters, and even tiles for a wall, backsplash, or shower. Painting bisqueware is almost as direct as painting on paper, canvas, wood, or any other material, and that's part of its appeal. You can have fun playing with color and pattern in a direct manner, or explore decorative painting techniques like stenciling, faux marbling, and rubber stamping; I'll show you these and many more methods for applying color to bisqueware. All the materials you need are readily available via your local contemporary studio, ceramics supplier, or mail order, so you can easily get started exploring the wonderful possibilities.

"Paint-your-own," or contemporary, ceramics studios, where ready-made bisqueware and studio time for decorating it are sold, began to proliferate in the 1990s, making pottery painting accessible to anyone with a little time and a creative urge and transforming it into the popular hobby and party activity it is today. This has prompted manufacturers and suppliers of ceramic colors, bisqueware, tools, and equipment to rise to the challenge of providing user-friendly products in ever-increasing variety, spurring hobbyists and professionals alike to approach decorating ceramics with a greater sense of play and experimentation, and thus helping to bring this medium into its own as a true art form.

At a contemporary ceramics studio you'll be offered a variety of bisque pottery pieces to choose from, along with an array of decorating colors, called underglazes, brushes and other tools for decorating, and plenty of instruction and inspiration to get you started on this exciting creative endeavor. When you've decorated your piece, the studio will glaze and fire it for you, and you can pick it up usually within a few days.

If you have some experience decorating ceramics and are considering setting up your own studio, this book will give you all the information you need on buying bisqueware and decorating materials. In your own studio you also have the responsibility of glazing and firing your work, so I've provided information on clear glazes and how to apply them, as well as what you need to know about purchasing and setting up a kiln, with a further section that guides you through the firing process. In your own work space you have the freedom to experiment with materials and methods that may not be

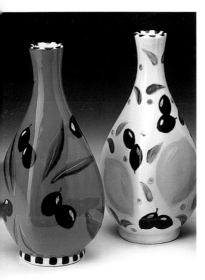

BOTTLES, HEIGHT 9"
(22.9 CM) EACH.

TWO PLATTERS,
11" (27.9 CM) SQUARE EACH.

available in a contemporary studio. For that reason I've included a chapter that introduces you to working with colored glazes, which ordinarily are not offered at a studio, as well as some postfiring decorative techniques.

If you're not ready to set up your own studio but wish to work more independently, many contemporary studios offer a kit of materials with which you can work at home, and will then glaze and fire your piece. For a fee, some studios will even fire pieces made from materials you've purchased elsewhere. Call your local contemporary studio for information on its policies regarding firing service.

Although this book addresses the surface treatment of ready-made bisqueware, all the techniques I present are applicable to wheel-thrown or hand-built ceramics, as long as they are made with white earthenware clay, and the glaze firing is at the appropriate temperature.

If you're an experienced potter considering decorating bisqueware or seek inspiration for surface treatment of your handmade pottery, this book will be an invaluable companion. The realm of commercial decorating materials, both underglazes and glazes, can be very exciting to a potter accustomed to formulating his or her own materials, and they leave plenty of room for experimentation.

There are many practical advantages to using ready-made bisqueware and decorating materials, rather than hand-forming pottery from wet clay and mixing your own colors and glazes from raw materials. For the novice, the availability of these commercial products makes the medium of decorating clean, smooth-surfaced wares with clear, bright colors completely accessible. For the experienced potter, working with commercial products eliminates the hazardous dust of raw materials from the studio and the need for a bisque firing before decorating or glazing your pieces, and saves a lot of time testing and developing colors and glazes.

I hope the material in this book will inspire you to look beyond basic painting techniques and help you express your own creative vision through the exciting medium of ceramics. You can dip your big toe in to test the water, or dive in head first. It's up to you!

KRISTEN MILLS, VASE, HEIGHT 9" (22.9 CM).

ARTICHOKE PLATTER, 4¹/₂ × 9" (11.4 × 22.9 CM).

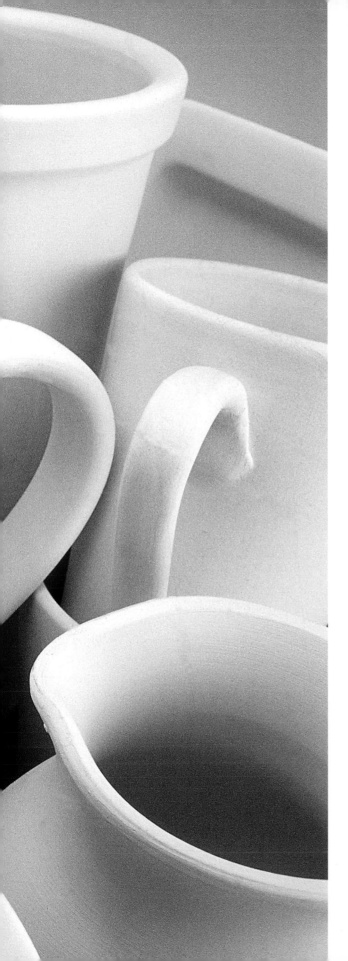

1

Getting Started: Materials and Methods

IN THIS CHAPTER I'll introduce you to the basic materials and methods used in painting, glazing, and firing bisque ceramics, taking you from start to finish so that you'll have an idea of the process as a whole. I'll cover specific decorating techniques in subsequent chapters.

If you're working in a contemporary studio, your pieces will be glazed and fired for you; however, if you're working independently, you'll need to know about glazing and firing procedures, so I've included all the essential information about these processes here. Even if you won't be glazing and firing your own work, it's useful to have at least a general understanding of these steps.

BISQUEWARE

BISQUEWARE is premade pottery or tile that has been fired once, leaving it hard and porous. This porosity is essential in that it makes it easy for the glaze or underglaze to adhere to the piece. In addition, this initial bisque firing gives the ware strength and durability; unfired pottery, known as greenware, is much more fragile. Once clay is bisque-fired,

it can no longer be wetted (or slaked) down into soft clay again.

The bisqueware available to the studio potter and in a contemporary ceramics studio is generally made of white earthenware and is intended to be fired at a relatively low temperature. (It's actually the clear glaze, or colored glazes if you're using them, that are most temperature specific. The ware itself will generally withstand the higher firing temperatures some kinds of glazes require; if you have your own studio you can experiment with these.) For the purposes of this book, we will assume we're firing in the lower range. (If you're working in a contemporary studio, you don't need to be concerned with firing temperature.) Lower firing temperature generally results in ware that is somewhat fragile. Compared to stoneware and porcelain, which are fired at temperatures a few hundred degrees hotter, earthenware requires careful handling to avoid chipping.

In a contemporary studio, you buy your bisqueware by the piece from the selection offered there. There's a much wider variety available to you if you're buying your own (see the source list in the appendices), but generally you will have to buy it by the case—which may contain anywhere from two to twenty-four pieces—and often meet minimum order requirements. However, you'll pay a lot less per piece this way. Sometimes suppliers will allow you to buy a small number of cases for a first order, or will even sell you a sample pack so you can try out their wares before committing to a larger order.

Some bisque suppliers also offer tiles, but if you are buying your own it's worth looking into suppliers that specialize in tiles for a greater variety of sizes and shapes, and for price comparison.

Miscellaneous bisqueware pieces.

UNDERGLAZES are the most accessible means of decorating bisqueware; think of them as paint for ceramics. You can mix colors and mix brands with similarly consistent results.

Besides brushes, tools for decorating bisqueware may include anything you might use for any type of decorative painting, such as sponges, stamps, stencils, and so forth. In the technique demonstrations given in chapters 3 and 4 I'll be introducing other tools as well. All of them are widely available and inexpensive.

There are a number of other materials, beyond underglazes, that you can use for decorating bisque. At the end of chapter 3, I discuss the majolica technique, in which you use a combination of colored glazes and modified underglazes to decorate white-glazed ware. In chapter 4 I'll introduce you to colored glazes, which are substantially different from underglazes and offer a wider variety of surface quality. I'll also show you another avenue to explore on non-dinnerware pieces—the use of nonfired materials such as acrylic paints and paper collage or découpage, which are applied after the firing to predetermined unglazed portions of the piece. Used in conjunction with fired colored glazes and underglazes, these nonfired materials offer yet more possibilities for rich and contrasting surface treatments.

Various materials and tools for underglazing techniques: underglazes in a range of colors, along with brushes, sponges, stencils, and stamps for applying them.

CLEAR GLAZES

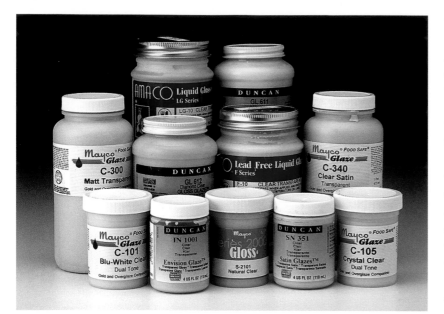

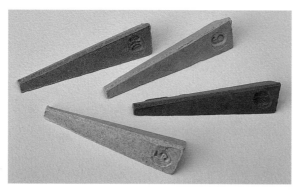

ABOVE: Clear glazes in gloss, satin, and matte finishes offered by various manufacturers.

RIGHT: Pyrometric cones.

Clear glaze tests. It's important to test a clear glaze over a range of colors, and useful to do so on a vertical surface (as I've done here) to determine whether it runs or pools toward the bottom of the piece.

CLEAR GLAZES are basically composed of silica (glass), alumina (so the glaze will adhere to the bisque surface), and various fluxes (chemicals that make the silica melt at a given temperature).

A clear glaze is applied over a bisque piece once it has been decorated with underglazes. Then the piece is fired. It is not necessary to fire the decorated piece before glazing. The label on the clear glaze will specify the temperature at which it should be fired, expressed as a cone number. That number refers to pyrometric cones, which are used to monitor firings and determine when a firing is finished. They are composed of ceramic materials determined to soften, and eventually melt, when a given amount of heat has been absorbed. Each cone number indicates a different amount of heat absorption required for the cone to soften, or bend. The higher the number, the more heat the cone must absorb. A zero (0) preceding a cone number functions like the minus sign in a negative number, such that cone 04 is hotter than cone 05. Cone 06 is usually indicated on low-fire glazes (as opposed to high-fire stoneware glazes), but most of these will produce good results at cone 05 or cone 04. I fire to cone 05. (For more information on firing, see the appendices at the back of this book.)

I tested twelve different clear glazes from five different manufacturers, including lead-bearing and lead-free gloss glazes, and a few satin matte clear glazes. The composition of the clear glaze does affect the fired color of the underglazes beneath, though the differences are minimal among commercially made clear glazes. The differences in raw working quality are more apparent— some are thinner in consistency, some dry more quickly, etc. Your choice of clear gloss glaze is a matter of personal preference. There is more obvious difference among satin matte (that is, flat rather than shiny) clear glazes, in both sheen and clarity, and in how they affect the underlying underglaze colors.

One consideration in choosing clear glazes is whether or not they contain lead. A small amount of lead in a clear glaze will promote a clarity and brilliance in underglaze colors not otherwise easily achieved. I prefer a lead-bearing glaze for this subtle effect on color and for its tolerance of minor firing temperature discrepancies (often a kiln will have "hot spots" and "cold spots"). Lead-bearing glazes smooth out over the surface of the bisque during firing, so that irregular brushstrokes (if you are brushing on your glaze) or drips will not show.

Because of the toxicity of lead in the raw glaze, most glaze manufacturers offer a lead-free clear glaze and one that contains just a small amount of lead, but that's dinnerware safe when fired correctly. Commercially made glazes are suspended in media that have adhesive qualities that prevent the formation of dust. When the glaze is dry, it won't powder off on your hands as you handle the piece, and won't become airborne for you to breathe. Thus, the lead does not present a respiratory hazard. However, it is important when using a lead-bearing glaze to be careful not to ingest it. Wash your hands and clean your work surface after glazing. Do not eat while glazing with a lead-bearing glaze. (See more safety precautions discussed in chapter 4.)

TOP RIGHT AND RIGHT: These pieces were glazed with a clear matte glaze, which results in a smooth, flat finish rather than the shiny quality produced by a clear glossy glaze.

BASIC PROCESS

THESE ARE THE BASIC STEPS that take you from your plain bisqueware and decorating materials to a finished piece. The materials you need are as follows:

- Bisqueware
- Wax resist, and a brush dedicated only for use with this material
- Underglazes and application tools (see chapter 3)
- Clear glaze
- Mop brush for applying clear glaze, or bucket for dipping
- Decorating wheel (not absolutely necessary, but very useful)
- Piece of foam rubber slightly bigger than the decorating wheel
- Paper towels

Step One: Wax Resist

Apply wax resist to the bottom of your bisqueware piece. If your piece has a foot ring rather than a flat bottom, you need only apply the wax resist to the bottom of the foot. This is to prevent any glaze from getting on the bottom of the ware; otherwise, it will stick to the kiln shelf during firing. The glaze melts during firing, and when it cools becomes a hard, glassy substance, fused to any surface with which it has come in contact. Underglaze does not melt in the kiln, so it's okay to get underglaze on the bottom of the piece. You can decorate the piece, including the bottom, and then apply the wax resist over the underglaze before glazing if you prefer. Wax resist is water miscible while wet, but once dry it will not wash off with water, becoming a waxy, impermeable barrier. So it's important to avoid getting it on any area of the piece you intend to decorate and glaze.

Step Two: Decorate with Underglazes

Decorate the piece with underglazes using any of the techniques described in chapter 3. Let the underglazes dry completely before moving on to the next step. Underglazes remain moist— but not wet the way paint does—soon after application, because the bisque's porous surface absorbs the water in their composition quickly. The colors lighten in the process and, until they're completely absorbed, will feel cool to the touch. Drying may take up to half a day or so depending on how warm and dry the ambient air is. Although technically it's not necessary to wait for underglazes to be totally dry before clear glazing, doing so makes the clear glaze application easier because the latter will dry more quickly between coats.

Applying wax resist to the foot ring of a plate I plan to glaze.

Step Three: Apply Clear Glaze

Coat the piece with a clear glaze. Glazing can be done either by brushing or dipping. Dipping is a lot faster, but brushing gives you more control and is subject to fewer problems. Many manufacturers offer their clear glazes in both brushing and dipping formulas; it's important to get the appropriate kind.

Brushing technique: First, pour your glaze into a wide-mouth container. I find a pint-size food storage container serviceable for this purpose. For a bowl or a plate I start with the piece upside down on the decorating wheel with a piece of foam supporting it, and a paper towel over the foam to protect the piece from any dirt. Using your mop brush, apply three even coats of glaze to the bottom of the piece, letting the glaze dry between each coat (drying usually takes about five to ten minutes). I use four decorating wheels and work on four pieces at once, applying the first coat to all four, then the second, etc. If you don't have more than one decorating wheel, you may want to begin working on another piece while waiting for the glaze to dry.

When the bottom is glazed with three coats, turn the piece over and repeat the process on the inside or top of the piece, taking care to apply glaze to the rim. Using a damp paper towel or sponge, gently remove any little droplets of glaze that may have gotten on the waxed foot.

For an upright piece such as a pitcher, mug, or vase, pick up the piece, glaze the bottom (except where there's wax resist on the foot) with three coats, then put the piece back down on the decorating wheel and glaze the inside (and handle, if any) with three coats, then proceed to glaze the sides.

Demonstration: BRUSHING TECHNIQUE

1 I apply three coats of clear glaze to the bottom of my underglaze-decorated plate, letting each coat dry between applications.

2 When the bottom is dry, I turn the plate over and repeat the process on the top.

3 Here I'm applying glaze to the rim.

Dipping technique: Glazes formulated for the dipping method are meant to be viscous enough to coat bisqueware in just one application, rather than those made for the brushing method, requiring three coats.

Pour glaze into a large container such as a plastic storage crate or bucket, to a depth at least one-half the diameter of the biggest object you will be glazing. Stir well with a clean toilet brush or a large whisk.

For a plate or bowl, dip the piece at least halfway into the glaze and lift it out quickly. Shake drips back into the glaze container. When this first application of glaze is dry, hold the piece by the glazed portion and dip the other half in the same manner, allowing the glaze to overlap the already glazed area just slightly. Remove any traces of glaze on the waxed foot or bottom of the piece.

For a mug, vase, or any other upright vessel, first, using a clean container such as a plastic cup or pitcher, pour glaze into the interior of the vessel, then pour the glaze back into the bucket as you gently turn the piece, so that the glaze coats the entire inside. Shake off the excess drips. Next, hold the bottom of the piece and dip it at least halfway into the glaze. In this step it is important to hold the piece *vertically*, rather than at an angle, so that the air trapped inside the piece will push the surface of the glaze down, preventing you from reglazing the inside. Remove the piece and let excess glaze drip back into the bucket, then allow the glaze to dry. Then, holding the top, glazed portion, dip the bottom half into the glaze, allowing it to overlap the previously glazed portion slightly. Again, wipe the waxed bottom or foot ring to remove any glaze.

Demonstration: DIPPING TECHNIQUE—PLATE OR BOWL

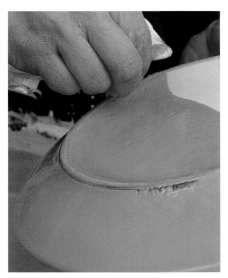

1 I dip my plate into the bucket of glaze and coat it at least halfway, lifting it out quickly and shaking drips of glaze back into the container.

2 When the first application is dry I hold the piece by the glazed portion and dip the other half as before, letting the glaze slightly overlap the already coated area.

3 I then remove any traces of glaze on the waxed bottom of the piece.

Demonstration: DIPPING TECHNIQUE—UPRIGHT CONTAINER

1 I use a clean plastic cup to pour glaze into my mug.

2 I then pour the glaze back into the bucket, gently turning the piece so glaze coats the entire inside. I shake off excess drips.

3 Holding the piece by the bottom, I dip it at least halfway into the glaze. It's important to hold the piece *vertically* rather than at an angle in this step; you want the air trapped inside the piece to push the surface of the glaze down so you don't reglaze the inside.

4 I let excess glaze drip back into the bucket.

5 After allowing the glaze to dry, I hold the piece by the top, glazed part and dip the bottom half into the glaze, letting it slightly overlap the previously glazed portion.

6 I wipe the bottom where it has been waxed to remove any glaze.

Step Four:
Load the Kiln

Glazed bisqueware pieces are loaded in the kiln on a series of shelves separated by kiln posts. *Kiln shelves* may be half-round in shape or angular sided; they are made of a dense, strong refractory material, usually silicon carbide, and last a very long time so can be used repeatedly. *Kiln posts,* also reusable, come in different heights to accord with the height of the pieces you're firing.

Kiln post with a pyrometric cone placed horizontally atop it.

I apply kiln wash to a kiln shelf; only one coat is needed, and only on the top of the shelf. It's not necessary to wait for the wash to dry before placing shelves in the kiln.

The first step is to apply a coat of kiln wash to the top side of the shelves. Composed of silica and alumina, kiln wash prevents accidental glaze drips from sticking to the kiln shelf or the bottoms of bisqueware pieces.

The next step is to place four short kiln posts in equidistant corners directly on the bottom of the kiln, then set a pair of shelves on those posts. All subsequent layers of kiln posts should align with the bottommost posts, and the first set of posts added after the bottom layer should be just a little taller than the tallest piece you will put on that shelf layer.

Place your glazed pieces on the shelves, making sure that they do not touch one another or the kiln posts. For efficiency, load pieces of similar height together on one shelf layer. Place another pair of kiln-washed shelves on the four posts, and then another set of four posts. The number of layers of firing-ready wares you can accommodate depends on the height of your pieces and the size of the kiln; for example, flat wares like tiles or plates take up much less space than vases or other tall objects.

During this process, place each of your pyrometric cones horizontally on a separate, short kiln post at the edge of the kiln shelf so that you can see them through a spy hole about halfway up the side of the kiln. For more accurate monitoring, you may want to place cones in the lower and upper portions of the kiln as well; kilns usually have at least three spy holes so you can check temperature variations in different areas. Close the lid of the kiln and fire. (For more information on kilns and firing, as well as more details on kiln loading, see the appendices at the back of this book.)

Demonstration: LOADING THE KILN

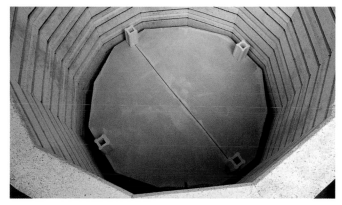

1 After placing four short kiln posts in equidistant corners at the bottom of the kiln, I set a pair of shelves atop them, then position a second set of posts directly over those underneath. This set of posts should be just a little taller than the tallest piece you intend to put on that shelf layer.

2 I place my glazed pieces on the shelf layer, making sure they don't touch one another or any of the kiln posts. It's best to load pieces of similar height on a given shelf layer.

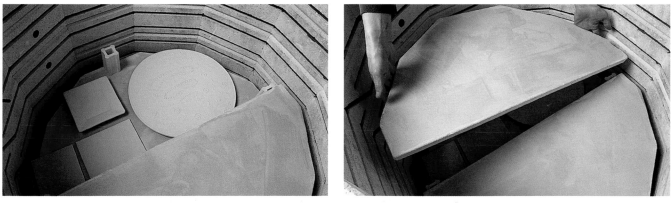

3 I position another layer of shelves. The number of shelf layers will depend on the kiln size and on the height of the pieces being fired.

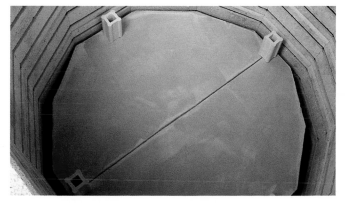

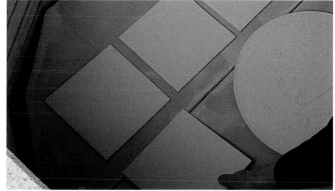

4 I then position another layer of posts aligning with those below.

5 You don't need to put a shelf layer over the final layer of pieces; just make sure they don't protrude above the top of the kiln.

2

Color, Form, and Design

THE MOST IMPORTANT THING in choosing colors or creating a design is to follow your own sense of what looks right. Trust your intuition. The following discussion is meant to give you a framework within which you can explore your own tastes and preferences. There are no rules about which colors go together, how to approach a particular bisqueware form, or how to create a pattern or design. If you're intimidated by the overwhelming range of possibilities and need a starting point, or feel you're stuck in a rut of using the same colors and design approaches repeatedly, then this chapter may be useful before you start. If, on the other hand, you already have some ideas you want to try, but need information on application techniques, skip this chapter for now and use it for reference as needed.

COLOR

THE MAJOR CHARACTERISTICS of color are hue, value (or tone), saturation, and temperature (or mood), all terms used in any discussion of color theory. My intention in presenting the basics of color theory here is to make you more aware of your own personal reactions to color, and to establish a common vocabulary for talking about it. In making color choices the bottom line is what appeals to you. If some color or color combination doesn't look good to you, or looks slightly off, an understanding of how colors relate to one another can be useful in determining how to correct it. Color theory is not a set of rules governing which colors may be used together. Only you can determine that. Rather, it's a body of information that can help you identify and articulate your own color sense.

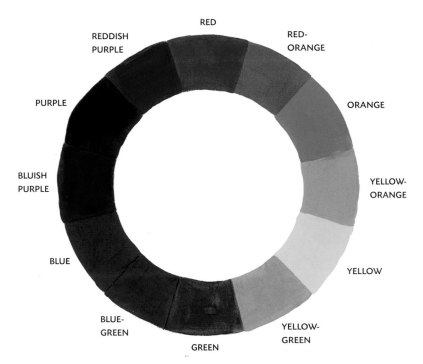

A typical color wheel showing primary colors: red, blue, and yellow; secondary colors: orange, green, and purple; and tertiary colors: yellow-orange, red-orange, reddish purple, bluish purple, blue-green, and yellow-green.

Hue

Hue is the characteristic of color that identifies it by name. "Red," "blue," "green," and so on refer to hue.

Primary colors are so called because they cannot be mixed from any other colors. They are the building blocks, or the basis, for all other colors. (In theory this is the case, since we are speaking of hypothetical pure color; actual pigments and the mediums in which they are suspended, however, can produce a variety of results when mixed, so it is always necessary to test them.) Red, blue, and yellow are the three primary colors, and they are placed equidistant on a color wheel, a device for illustrating relationships among colors. *Secondary colors* are those mixed from two primaries: green is mixed from yellow and blue; orange from yellow and red; purple from red and blue. Secondary colors are placed between the primaries from which they are mixed on the color wheel. *Tertiary colors* are those in between primaries and secondaries: red-orange, blue-green, yellow-green, and so forth.

Analogous color schemes.

Colors adjacent to each other on the color wheel are called *analogous colors*. Red and orange, for example, are analogous, and so are red and red-orange. "Analogous" is to some extent a matter of degree. Red and yellow-orange could be considered analogous, but a slightly bluish red, tending toward reddish purple, would not be considered analogous with yellow-orange. In practice, analogous colors are a good place to start if you're unsure of a color scheme. If you're not yet familiar with putting colors together, colors close on the color wheel will almost always blend harmoniously.

Complementary colors are those opposite each other on the color wheel. Red and green are complementary; so are blue and orange, and yellow and purple. These complementary pairs consist of a primary color and the secondary color made up of the remaining two primaries. But tertiary colors also have complements: reddish purple is opposite yellow-green on the color wheel, for example, and they form a complementary pair. The same is true of bluish purple and orange-yellow. Pairs of complementary colors have special properties that are important to your understanding of color mixing and choosing a color scheme.

When a color is placed next to its complement, both colors tend to appear more intense, even to vibrate or clash. In creating a pattern or an image, adding just a touch of a color that is complementary to the main color can add interest. However, complementary colors used in approximately equal measure can seem to compete with each other, as illustrated by the two plates below.

Pairs of complementary colors: orange and blue, green and red, purple and yellow, yellow-green and reddish purple, yellow-orange and bluish purple, blue-green and red-orange.

LEFT: **LIZARD AVOCADO PLATTER, DIAMETER 16" (40.6 CM).** RIGHT: **YELLOW PEPPER PLATE, DIAMETER 12" (30.5 CM).**
These two plates show how complementary colors used in nearly equal amounts in a design can seem to compete with each other.

Another important property of complementary colors is that mixing a pair of them in approximately equal amounts produces a dull brown, or "mud." This is useful to know for two reasons: first, to

keep your colors fresh and bright, avoid mixing complementaries. On the other hand, to decrease the intensity of a color, or "neutralize" it, you can add a tiny bit of its complement. To lessen the intensity of a bright yellow, for example, add just a touch of purple. In the color wheel shown at left, I created the inner circle by adding a bit of the complement to each of the primary, secondary, and tertiary colors. Theoretically the center of the color wheel would be completely neutral—no particular color at all. However, if you want to include neutral colors such as beige, taupe, etc., in your palette, you will get the most consistent results by buying them rather than mixing them.

Value

Value (sometimes called *tone*) refers to the relative lightness or darkness of a color. Adding white to a color produces lighter values, or *tints*, while adding black produces darker values, or *shades*. It's useful to make value scales from light to dark of the underglaze colors you use. It's easiest to do this on a flat surface such as a tile. First, put about a teaspoon of an unmixed underglaze color in each of two small plastic cups. Brush a square of the pure color onto a test tile in the middle of what will be the value sequence.

To create lighter values of a pure color, in one of the cups, mix in just a bit of white underglaze to the original, unmixed color to make your first tint, and brush a square of the result right below the pure color. Add another bit of white to the same cup to create a lighter tint and brush the result immediately underneath the previous one on the tile, and so forth, until you have perhaps three gradations of lightness. To create darker values, in the other cup of pure

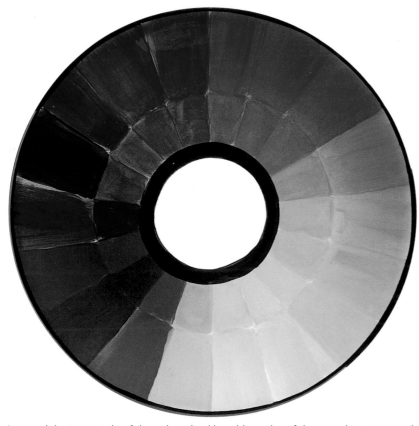

I created the inner circle of this color wheel by adding a bit of the complement to each of the primary, secondary, and tertiary colors; note the neutralizing effect this produces.

Value scales of underglaze colors.

color mix in just a bit of black underglaze in a similar sequential fashion. Usually this calls for much less black than the additions of white you use to make tints; start with about a drop of black and proceed from there to produce perhaps three gradations of shade.

The amount of white or black you need to add to a pure color to create tints and shades depends partly on the brand and quality of the underglazes you're using. For darker values of some colors, in general I prefer to buy underglazes in those shades already produced by the manufacturer, as the addition of black to a pure color seems to affect the hue more than does the addition of white.

Doing a quick value scale of a specific underglaze color gives you information on the tinting strength of that underglaze (more on this in chapter 3) and on color possibilities. If you want to make a larger quantity of a color that you've mixed for your value scales, you can measure more carefully to determine a reliable recipe. You could be very scientific about this and do exact measurements, keeping accurate records, but I find that eyeballing the results goes much faster and is, for my own purposes at least, adequate.

If you're unsure about what color scheme to establish in a design, as with analogous colors, another safe place to start is to use several different values of one color. The plates and tiles pictured at right were each decorated with one color straight from the jar, one tint of that color (mixed with white), and one shade (the pure color mixed with black).

TOP TO BOTTOM: **FLOWER, BIRD, AND FISH PLATES, DIAMETER 10" (25.4 CM) EACH.**
These plates and tiles were decorated using three values of the same color: one straight from the jar, one tint of that color, and one shade.

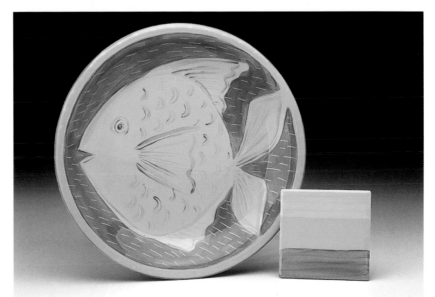

The top row of tiles shows pure colors at full saturation, while in the bottom row the same hues have been neutralized by the addition of another color, and are thus less intense.

These tiles show warm and cool versions of four different colors. The colors on the left side of the tiles look warm to me, while those on the right side look cool.

Saturation

Saturation is the relative intensity, or brightness, of a color. A saturated color will stand out against a less saturated one. An underglaze straight out of the jar is the most saturated it will get. That is, you can't intensify a color by adding another one—black, white, or any other hue—to it; doing so will lower its intensity. The exception is that adding a more saturated color to a less-saturated version of the same hue—for example, adding a bright yellow to a dull yellow—will brighten the dull yellow. In the sample tiles shown at left you can see how the slightly neutralized colors in the bottom row appear less intense than their pure counterparts above.

Warm and Cool Colors

Color temperature, or as it's sometimes called, "mood," is a bit subjective; perceptions may depend on personal reactions or on the context in which a particular color is seen. Generally, though, warm colors are those associated with the sun, fire, heat—reds, oranges, yellows—while cool colors are those associated with the ocean and the like—greens, blues, purples. With that as a basis of comparison, there are warm and cool versions of any color. To some extent we can identify warmer and cooler colors in terms of their placement on the color wheel. For example, a warm red is one that tends toward orange, while a cool red tends toward purple. A cool yellow may be slightly greenish, whereas a warm yellow is one with a touch of orange. Value and saturation also play a role in our perception of colors as warm or cool, as does context.

Color in Context

I hope it's clear from the previous examples that colors are related to one another in particular ways. You may be able to describe an individual color adequately in terms of hue, saturation, value, and temperature, but these characteristics become much more apparent, and more meaningful, when you put an individual color within a specific context or color scheme. Take a look at the examples shown here to see how this works.

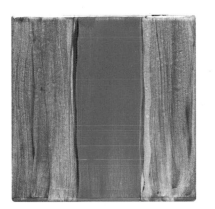

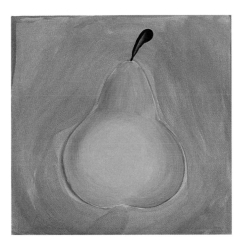

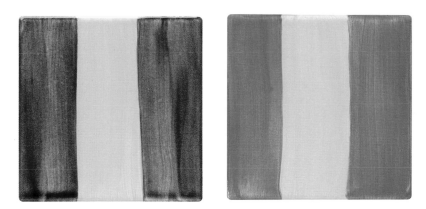

In the top pair of tiles, notice how the red looks different depending on whether it is flanked by blue or by orange. The same is true for the blue and the yellow, respectively, in the other examples shown here.

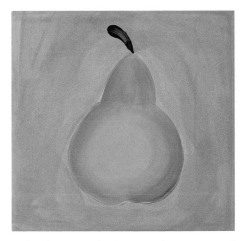

In the tile at top, the pear stands out against the cool green background, whereas it competes with the warm yellow-green background in the bottom example.

Raw and glazed and fired underglazes.

After applying underglaze colors to a tile, while they are still damp I scratch an identification code into them with a knitting needle. I then glaze and fire the piece and use it for reference.

Raw and Fired Color

When glazed and fired, all your underglaze colors become much more intense and brilliant than they look in the jar. (If you were to fire the underglazes without a clear glaze over them, they would still look more or less as they do in the jar, as the materials that make up the color in underglazes are prefired.) A contemporary ceramics studio will have fired samples of all the colors it offers. If you're working in your own studio it's a good idea to glaze and fire sample tiles of each underglaze in your palette for easy reference. Identify each tile either on the back with an underglaze pencil, or on the color itself using the sgraffito technique (see page 65); I use a knitting needle for this, scratching into the underglaze color while it's slightly damp. I use the manufacturer's code number for identification, but you can use any code that makes sense to you. As you gain familiarity with your colors you may not need to refer to the fired samples as much, and do the visual translation in your head. But the samples will remain useful for creating new color combinations.

Color Mixing

To mix a solid, even color, the way to achieve the most consistent and uniform results is to follow the procedure given for the color wheel and value scale exercises. That is, mix the colors thoroughly in a separate container with a brush. However, you can also mix colors directly on the bisque piece. In my own work there are very few colors that I mix prior to applying them to the bisque. I prefer to use several of the following methods, as they allow the colors to retain their freshness and brilliance.

Simple layering: This technique involves simply brushing one color over another. You can wait for the first layer to dry, or not. By letting the underglaze dry in between applications, you achieve a more uniform resulting color than if you apply the different colors while still wet. Also, by letting the first color dry, the piece will absorb more of the second color, resulting in a more saturated final color. However, I prefer to mix colors while they are wet for most of my work, because it allows them to remain fresh and bright. I think of this method in terms of a base coat as the main color, and subsequent colors as modifiers. For instance, I may brush on a base coat of orange, then loosely apply a yellow and then a peach over it, as I'm doing in the example shown below. By "loosely" I mean brushing the yellow and peach in a manner that leaves streaks of each color, rather than smooth, even coats. Your eye perceives these as one color or area of color.

LEFT: After brushing on a base coat of orange, while it's still wet, I loosely apply a yellow and a peach over it, leaving streaks of each color.

BELOW: The tile at left was painted first with orange, then with yellow over it while the orange was still wet, whereas in the tile in the center, the yellow was applied after the orange was dry. The tile at right was done using the simple "wet-on-wet" color layering method.

Gradation: A gradation can be achieved by using the above method, working quickly so the underglazes remain moist. After applying the base coat of a mid-range color, brush a lighter color to one side of the area, a darker color to the other side, and if you wish, a little more of the base color to the middle to blend the two. This method depends on quick, confident strokes, so you may want to practice on a test tile or on paper before applying the underglazes to your piece.

You can also combine colors by sponging or drybrushing one or more colors over the base coat, as shown in some of the examples on page 31. I'll describe these techniques in the next chapter. These methods keep the colors more separate so that they retain their brilliance, but are perceived as one color.

Demonstration: CREATING A GRADATION

1 To create a gradation, first I brushed on a mid-range color (in this case orange); working while it's still wet, here I'm applying a lighter color (yellow) on one side.

2 Now I'm adding a darker color (peach) to the other side.

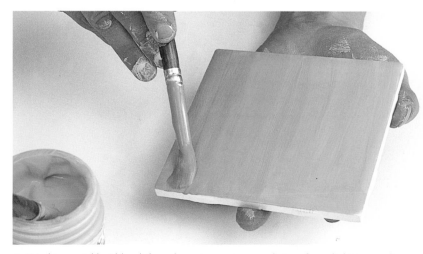

3 Working quickly, I blend these hues to create a gradation from light to medium to dark.

4 The tile after firing.

Developing a Palette

If you are buying your first set of under-glazes, or choosing from those provided by a studio, I recommend getting at least two versions of each of the six major colors—red, orange, yellow, green, blue, and purple. Don't worry about matching the hues on the color wheel. It is, after all, a theoretical device for helping you classify and talk about color. Choose colors you like. If you hate red-orange, find another red that you prefer. But if you hate reds altogether, select one or two anyway (ones that you dislike least), because they may serve to complement or show off colors that you do like; besides, you can use them for mixing and modifying other colors. Also, you'll want a black and a white. In addition to these, choose a few more colors that strike your fancy if your budget, or the studio, allows. If your budget is con-strained, one of each color plus black and white should suffice. It is important to start with a full range in order to gain an understanding of color and to develop your own palette.

The colors you begin with and those you mix from them constitute your palette. Each person's palette will reflect his or her personal preferences, and most likely won't look like the theoretical color wheel. As you gain experience and develop your own sense of color, your palette will change. Fortunately you can buy underglazes in small quantities—they're available in four-ounce and even two-ounce jars—so you can try a lot of different colors without buying huge amounts.

A *color scheme* is a group of colors you choose from your palette for a particular project. You may find yourself falling into the habit of using the same color scheme on every piece. Using the same group of colors repeatedly gives you a deeper understanding of how those colors work together in varying propor-tions and design contexts. However, it's also fun to challenge yourself by adding a color you wouldn't ordinarily use, or by subtracting a color that you find yourself relying on constantly. A basic rule of thumb when creating your palette and choosing a color scheme is, first go with your gut feelings—use colors that look right to you. Then every once in a while convince yourself to try something new.

Examples of other color mixing methods.

FORM

FOR ANY PIECE of bisque you choose to decorate, it's important first to notice its parts, or analyze its anatomy. A three-dimensional ceramic form is not a flat canvas. Some pieces can be treated more or less as two-dimensional surfaces—tiles or decorative platters, for example—but for the most part, painting bisqueware demands attention to form.

An *articulation* of form is simply a transition point in the shape: the point at which a handle meets the body of a mug, the angle where a vase flares out. Articulations can be sharp or abrupt like a corner, or they can be gentler and less clearly defined, like a change in the direction of a curve.

A plate, for example, may have a distinctly articulated rim, or it may be flat except for a gentle curve at the edge. In the first case, you may choose to emphasize the distinction between rim and center by decorating each part differently. Or you may wish to deemphasize this articulation by decorating it in one continuous pattern.

If you decide to ignore a particular articulation of any piece, it should be a

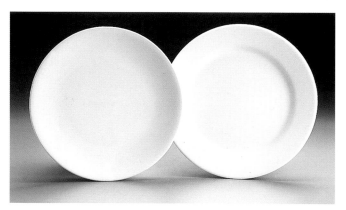

The bisqueware plate at left is essentially flat except for the gentle upward curve at its edge, while the one on the right has a distinctly articulated rim.

GREEN FOLIAGE PLATE, DIAMETER 12" (30.5 CM).
Here I've deemphasized the plate's articulation by decorating it in one continuous pattern.

ABOVE TOP: **OLIVE PLATE, DIAMETER 12" (30.5 CM).**
ABOVE: **SUSAN KRAMER, PLATE, DIAMETER 12" (30.5 CM).**
These two examples illustrate how decoration can be used to emphasize the different parts of a form, the distinction in this case being between the rim and center of each plate.

conscious choice, as if you were to say to yourself, "Look, I can make this pattern (or image) go all over the pot like a skin" or "See how this form distorts this image."

When choosing a bisque piece, examine it and ask the following questions: Is the object's profile made up of curves, or straight lines? Are the curves gentle or sharp? Are they continuous, or do they change direction? Is there more than one continuous curve or line? Is the form concave, or convex? Where is the volume? Does it have a distinct foot, or does the form stop abruptly where it sits on the table? If it is a bowl, is it wide, shallow, and open, or is it more upright and inward-curving? If your piece is square or rectangular, are the corners sharp or rounded? Look at the various examples shown here to get yourself thinking about these qualities.

The point is that the shape of a piece, its anatomy and form, can inform or inspire your approach to decorating it. You can simply draw a picture or paint a design on a pot, but what makes decorating bisqueware interesting and challenging (and ultimately results in better pieces) is integrating the surface design with the form.

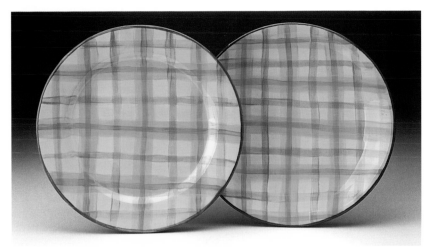

ABOVE TOP: **PLAID PLATES, DIAMETER 10" (25.4 CM) EACH.** In the plate at left the plaid pattern is distorted a little at the rim articulation, while in the example at right, the pattern fits smoothly over the plate's gently curved edge.

ABOVE: **FIVE-PIECE PLATE SET; LARGE PLATE, 13" (33 CM) SQUARE, SMALL PLATES, 5¹/₂" (14 CM) SQUARE EACH.** In this five-piece set, the sides and center of each plate are strongly articulated with solid, bold colors.

LEFT: **HEXAGONAL CHILE PLATES, DIAMETER 9" (22.9 CM) EACH.** In the plate at left, the decoration of the rim emphasizes the form's articulation, while the overall pattern on the plate at right ignores it.

When choosing a bisque piece, examine its anatomy; look at the examples shown here and consider the pieces' various angles, curves, lines, and so forth, and think about different decorative approaches that might be appropriate to these forms.

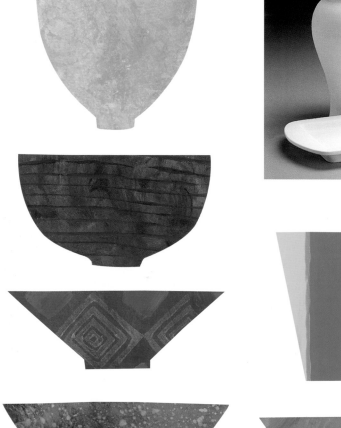

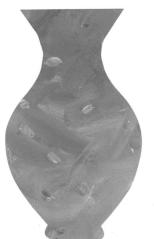

DESIGN

ANYTHING THAT VISUALLY inspires
you can be used as a design source, or
for developing a color scheme: a swatch
of fabric, a landscape, a food label, a
photograph, a painting, a piece of china,
a butterfly, a bird, a rug, your cat's mark-
ings, someone else's painted pottery, or
just an idea in your head with no particular reference. Though it is important
not to copy someone else's work and call
it your own, it's perfectly appropriate to
use another's work as a source of inspiration. The more you become involved in
painting bisqueware, the more you will
find yourself sensitive to visual stimuli.
It's useful to keep a sketchbook of ideas
and perhaps a file for clippings from
magazines, catalogs, and photos that
inspire you.

Another approach is to let the activity
of painting or drawing fuel your creative
urges. In the following chapter I discuss
a variety of underglaze application techniques using a number of different tools,
but you can play with these methods
using cheap paint on paper before committing to the bisqueware so as not to be
concerned with the expense of ceramic
materials. The images or patterns that
emerge from this kind of exercise may
generate design ideas.

ABOVE RIGHT: Sketches, illustrations from books or
magazines, patterns found in nature—these and
almost anything else can serve as inspiration for
your designs.

RIGHT: Playing with paint on paper is a good, inexpensive way to stimulate your visual creativity
before decorating a bisqueware piece.

Here's a leaf motif organized in three different ways on objects of various shapes and sizes; you can also vary the scale of a pattern according to the size of the motif in relation to the piece you're decorating.

RIGHT: **GEORGANNA (JANNO) GAY, "CHELSEA MORNING" DESSERT PLATE, DIAMETER 8"** (20.3 CM).

RIGHT BELOW: **GEORGANNA (JANNO) GAY, "ORIENT EXPRESS" OVAL PLATTER, 13 × 16" (33 × 40.6 CM).** The pattern on the plate at right is an example of dense coverage, while the pattern coverage on the platter below it is sparser.

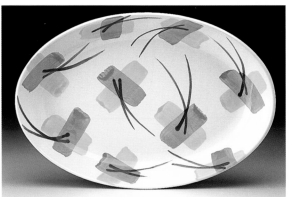

BELOW LEFT AND RIGHT: Stripes and plaids are simple but very appealing motifs to use in designing bisqueware pieces; the patterns can be arranged tightly or loosely.

Pattern

Pattern is basically an overall design consisting of a motif repeated in an organized way. The motif can be anything, from a simple line or brushstroke to an elaborate picture. It can be arranged in a random-looking, "tossed" manner, a tightly controlled and measured manner, or anywhere in between, as illustrated by the examples shown in this section. You can vary the scale of a pattern in terms of the size of motif in relation to the piece you're decorating. Another factor to consider is *coverage*, which refers to the density of the pattern, or how much space the motif occupies in relation to the background.

One easy approach that doesn't call for much drawing skill is to use line as a motif, whether in stripes or plaids; these can be tightly or loosely arranged. Likewise, you can use a simple square as a motif to make a checkerboard or an allover tossed pattern, or place the squares in a series of rows. Stamping and stenciling are particularly well suited to repeating a motif as well, and using brushstrokes in repeated sequences is a fun and easy way to explore pattern, too. We'll explore many patterning techniques in the next chapter.

Here are a few examples using a simple square as a motif in various patterns.

Stamping and stenciling are particularly well suited to repeating a motif, as these tiles illustrate.

Using brushstrokes in repeated sequences is a fun and easy way to explore pattern, as I've done on these mugs and tiles.

SUSAN STEINBERG (© STEINBERG DESIGNS LLC), PLATE, DIAMETER 9" (22.9 CM).

Here's an example of how another artist uses repeated brushstrokes to create not so much a pattern as an image.

Line

Line—the kind of graphic mark made with a brush or drawing tool—can be used in several ways. For example, you can use line to emphasize or define a motif, as with outlining. You can use it to articulate form, such as around the rim of a plate or at the point where the rim becomes distinct from the center, or to emphasize where a curve on a form changes direction. Line can also function as the motif itself, as in the striped and plaid decorations shown in the previous section. The quality of line can be as various as the quality of brushstrokes—loose and not precisely defined; clean and controlled; tentative; or bold and broad. Take a look at the illustrations shown here to see a few of the effective ways line can be used in design.

Visual Texture

My definition of visual texture is actually a form of pattern, and involves using two or more hues to add interest to a background or large area of color. I often use two closely related colors to create a texture that will add interest or dimension to an allover design; for sharper or deeper texture, you can use colors that contrast with each other. The tiles at bottom right on page 39 include small dots placed in a random pattern close together; an allover, sometimes random, sometimes regular, pattern applied with sponges; and drybrush applications of one color over another.

HARLEQUIN PLATE, DIAMETER 12" (30.5 CM).
I used line in various contexts on this plate: to define its outer edge (in green), the area where the form is demarcated by a rim (in orange), and around the diamond shapes of the interior pattern (in white).

SUSAN STEINBERG (© STEINBERG DESIGNS LLC), PIE PLATE, DIAMETER 11" (27.9 CM).
The bold black brushstrokes within and surrounding this floral motif both articulate its shapes and provide pleasing contrast against the white background.

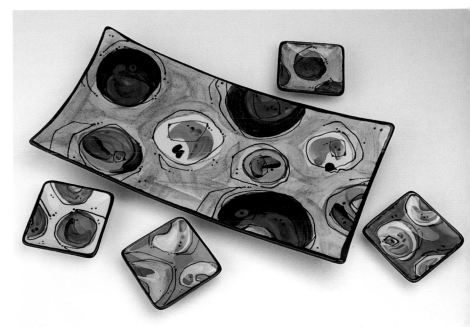

POPPY VASE, HEIGHT 11" (27.9 CM).
The black line just under the red rim of this vase emphasizes where the curve on the form changes direction.

KRISTEN MILLS, SUSHI PLATTER SET; SERVING PLATTER, 8 × 13" (20.3 × 33 CM); SAUCE DISHES, 3" (7.6 CM) SQUARE.
Note here how the artist Kristen Mills has used thin black outlines to emphasize the motifs of her design.

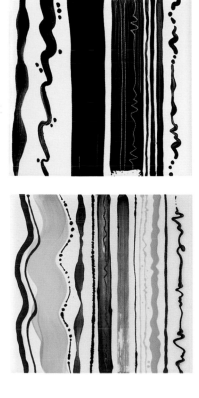

FAR LEFT: A few of the effective ways line can be used in design; these examples are by artist Kristen Mills.

LEFT: Examples of visual texture that can add interest to large areas of color or backgrounds.

3

Underglaze Techniques

THIS CHAPTER BEGINS with an in-depth discussion of underglazes—composition, basic properties like color, opacity, tinting strength, and brushing consistency, and how to choose those appropriate to your work. I then demonstrate numerous techniques for applying underglaze colors to bisqueware. If you've done any decorative painting, some of these techniques may already be familiar to you. But don't worry if you have no experience; anyone can paint ceramics! If you're a beginner, start with the simple brushstroke exercises. As you'll see, just about all the other application methods are equally accessible.

For most techniques, you don't have to wait till a color is completely dry before moving on to a subsequent step; usually it's sufficient to let it become dry to the touch, which takes only minutes because the bisque surface is porous and absorbs water in the underglaze fairly quickly. The undercoat color will remain somewhat moist for several hours, enhancing the flow of an additional color application over it. However, there are a few exceptions that call for an underglaze layer to be totally dry before you add more color to avoid lifting or otherwise disturbing the base coat; these include rubber stamping, some kinds of stenciling, and transfer techniques. It can take many hours for an underglaze application to dry completely, depending on atmospheric conditions, but to speed the process you can apply heat with a hairdryer or place your piece in a warm, dry spot, such as on or next to the kiln while a firing is in progress.

WHAT IS UNDERGLAZE?

UNDERGLAZES ARE ceramic colors in liquid form that are applied to bisqueware or greenware and typically glazed with a clear glaze before firing. The raw materials used as coloring agents in underglazes are metallic compounds such as oxides, carbonates, and sulfates. For example, cobalt compounds are used to make blues, chromium for greens, vanadium for yellows, and so forth. There are hundreds of such compounds and combinations available to manufacturers for producing a broad spectrum of colors.

In the manufacture of underglazes these coloring agents are often modified with opacifying agents such as zinc, tin, or zirconium, and then combined with a flux (a metallic oxide that promotes ceramic fusion or melting by interacting with the other oxides in the mixture), and with enough of a refractory material, usually silica or alumina, to keep the colorant from melting into the glaze applied over it. These materials are calcined, that is, fired in a crucible to the point at which they fuse together, or sinter, and are then ground very finely to create a ceramic stain. To make an underglaze this stain is combined with a medium that will give it a brushing consistency, keep the stain particles in suspension, and allow good adherence to the bisque surface.

Factors Affecting the Fired Color

Since the ceramic materials in the underglaze have already been fired, the color of the "raw" underglaze is the color that would result if you were to apply it to bisqueware and then fire it without a clear glaze. In most cases, especially in making dishes that will be used for food, we do apply a clear glaze over the underglaze before firing. This gives the ware a smooth, glassy surface and enhances the underglaze colors.

Another factor affecting the fired color of underglazes is firing temperature. Firing temperature is denoted in pyrometric cone numbers (see the appendices on kilns and firing for a detailed discussion). Generally, the most brilliant colors and broadest spectrum are achieved at lower temperatures, cone 06 to cone 04. Most commercially manufactured underglazes are intended for use at this temperature range, though many of them are stable at higher temperatures. I tested a spectrum of underglazes at cone 6 (using a clear glaze formulated for that temperature) and compared them to the same

BELOW TOP: Colored underglazes and clear glaze.

BELOW BOTTOM: I applied a clear glaze to the left half of each of these tiles but not to the right half, then fired them; note the difference between the glazed and unglazed color.

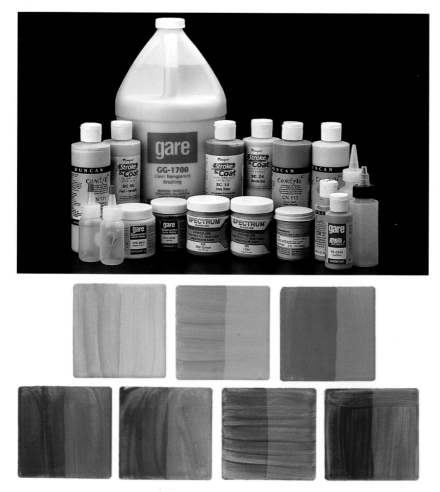

underglazes fired at cone 05 (cone 6 is approximately 300°F hotter than cone 05). As you can see in the examples at near right, the colors fired to the higher temperature (top) are less bright than those fired to the lower temperature, cone 05 (bottom). Ordinarily the directions on a jar of underglaze simply specify a cone number, usually cone 06, 05, or 04. The temperature difference within this range is relatively small, and will not make a significant color difference in your underglazes. I fire to cone 05, which is about 1890°F. For the purposes of this book, assume that, unless otherwise specified, we are firing to cone 05. All of the clear glazes that I tested produce good results at this temperature.

Choosing Underglazes

If you're setting up your own studio and buying your own underglazes, pay particular attention to my discussion below about how to test them for different characteristics and the factors affecting your choices.

On the other hand, if you're working in a contemporary ceramics studio, you'll be provided with underglazes, and the studio will have fired samples of all the available colors for reference so that you don't have to test them yourself in the ways I demonstrate here. Other characteristics such as opacity and translucency, tinting strength, and so on will become more evident once you've decorated several bisqueware pieces and seen the fired results. To gain a deeper understanding of underglazes, pay close attention to how many coats you apply; try mixing and layering colors, and make notes while you work. This helps you approach each new piece with a greater awareness of your materials and what to expect after firing.

Color

Color is the most obvious characteristic of an underglaze. Different manufacturers offer different varieties of color, and in developing your own palette you may want to use the products of several manufacturers. I use primarily Spectrum underglazes, but for color range I supplement them with underglazes made by Duncan, Amaco, Gare, and Mayco. Underglazes are usually available in very small quantities—two-ounce or four-ounce jars—so you can try a wide number. To test for color, I do a simple brush application of one, two, and three coats of each underglaze on a test tile, then glaze and fire it.

Opacity and Translucency

Opacity is the quality of not allowing light to go through, while translucency is the opposite, the quality of something through which you can see light. Underglazes are sometimes labeled "opaque" or "translucent," but almost any underglaze can be applied to produce a range of opacity and translucency, depending on how

LEFT, TOP AND BOTTOM: The tile at top was fired at cone 6; its colors are less bright than those on the tile below it, which was fired at the lower temperature of cone 05.

ABOVE: To test for color, I do a simple brush application of one, two, and three coats of each underglaze on a test tile, then glaze and fire it.

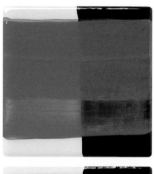
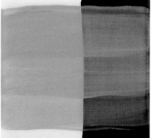

Opacity tests.

many coats you use or how much water you thin it with. To test translucency and opacity, paint a wide black underglaze stripe on a test tile and, when it's dry, apply one, two, and three coats of an underglaze over it, so that the color you are testing spans both black and white areas. Let each coat dry before applying the next one. In the raw state you may not be able to tell the difference between one coat and three. However, after firing with a coat of clear glaze, the difference can be dramatic.

The directions on the underglaze label will usually instruct you to apply three even coats, assuming you want opaque, even coverage. Exploiting the range of opacity and translucency of each underglaze gives you much more variety.

Tinting Strength

Tinting strength refers to the amount of color or pigment in a given volume of underglaze. "Tinting" refers to lightening color by adding white to it (see chapter 2). The more white you have to add to achieve a given tint, or value, the greater the color's tinting strength.

Most manufacturers produce a series of underglazes designed to have a higher pigment content, less "filler," and thus a higher tinting strength. These are generally more expensive than regular underglazes, but may be worth it if you are painting large areas or time-consuming details where you want opaque coverage. As with regular underglazes, these more concentrated ones vary in opacity and tinting strength from color to color, and from brand to brand.

To test tinting strength, proceed as for the value scales in chapter 2; see page 24. After glazing and firing you'll be able to see how much white it takes,

relative to the original color, to achieve a given tint. You then have an idea of how much pigment is in your underglaze.

I'm not suggesting that you test every underglaze meticulously for opacity and tinting strength before using it on a piece. You get a sense of these characteristics through repeated use. I do, however, suggest you test each underglaze for color, as described above. This will give you a sense of an underglaze's other qualities.

Workability/Brushing Consistency

The medium in which underglaze materials are suspended largely determines an underglaze's working qualities. Since bisqueware is porous, a liquid brushed on its surface can "dry," or be absorbed very quickly, limiting your control over its application. Most underglazes stay "wet," or unabsorbed, for a short time, allowing you to blend colors as you apply them, much like working in oil or acrylic paint. The more water that's in an underglaze (relative to the amount of medium), the more quickly it will be absorbed and dry on the bisque surface, making it more difficult to work with.

Besides the intensity of color, or tinting strength, the working quality of an underglaze is most likely to affect its price. Cheaper underglazes generally have poorer flowing quality, as they contain less medium and more water. Workability varies from brand to brand, but is usually consistent within the product line of a single manufacturer. Since I paint bisqueware for a living, and my time is the most valuable component of production, I personally choose to pay for top-quality underglazes that have good tinting strength and are easy to work with.

APPLICATION TECHNIQUES

MANY OF THE TECHNIQUES I show you here are common to decorative painting applications; stenciling and sponging, for example, are often used to embellish walls or furniture. Some of the other methods, like acetate transfer and spritzing/blotting, are approaches I've learned from making monotypes and watercolor paintings. Used in this context, these techniques can result in some unusual effects.

Most of the tools used in the following demonstrations will be provided by a contemporary studio. If you're interested in trying a particular technique in this setting, call ahead to see if the studio offers the appropriate tools; usually brushes, sponges, and stamps are available on premises, but some other materials, such as masking fluid, contact paper, and lace paper (as used in masking techniques), or acetate (as used in transfer techniques), may not be. However, ordinarily you're welcome to bring your own such items.

For the works shown on this page I used at least two of the application techniques described in this chapter, including brushing and sgraffito. Note that the designs in each grouping of objects employ three different motifs in coordinating colors.

Brushing

Brushing is the most common way of applying underglaze to bisqueware. It's a direct method, and brushes are familiar tools to most of us and are available in most studios.

There are many types of brushes, each designed for use with a specific medium or for a specific purpose. There are brushes for watercolor, oil, and acrylic painting, house painting, decorative painting, and so forth. Within each of these categories you'll find several different basic shapes, with variations, in a range of sizes. For decorating bisqueware, don't limit yourself to one type of brush, but experiment with a variety. You may ultimately settle on one or two types, and buy them in several sizes. In my studio I use mostly round watercolor brushes in three sizes, a few different flat brushes, and a mop brush for glazing. However, I keep some stiff-bristle brushes around (for drybrush techniques), sponge brushes, fan brushes, and a few others for experimenting.

Whatever types of brushes you choose, start by exploring the different kinds of marks you can make with each. Try loose, flowing brushstrokes as well as short, brisk ones. Try making stripes, circles, and lines with each brush. You can do this with paint on paper first to experiment and become familiar with each brush, or decorate a pot or a series of tiles as a "sampler" for visual reference.

ABOVE: An assortment of brushes.

RIGHT: Playing with different brushes and the kinds of marks they make.

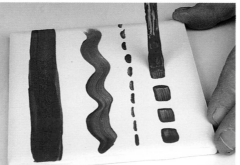

Demonstration: BRUSHING

In this demonstration, I create each
motif with a different type of brushstroke.
This is an easy way to get started.

1 Here I use a flat brush to create a checkerboard motif in a light violet blue hue on my small square plate.

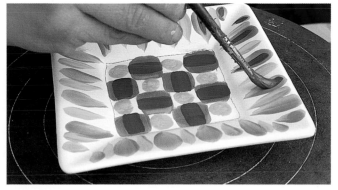

2 Next, I use a stencil brush to create dots of yellow between the pattern of squares.

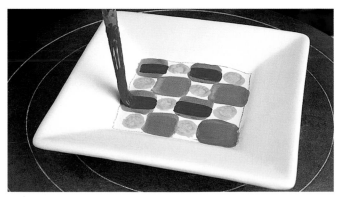

3 I use a smaller flat brush to add a darker blue to the square motif.

4 To decorate the rim of my plate, I use a round brush to apply teardrop-shape strokes in a light violet color.

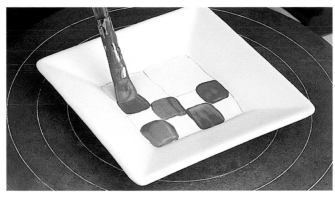

5 Now, with a smaller round brush, I apply yellow strokes between the light violet ones.

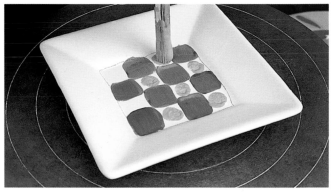

6 With another round brush I add a darker accent color to the violet strokes already established.

PLATE, 6" (15.2 CM) SQUARE.
The glazed and fired result.

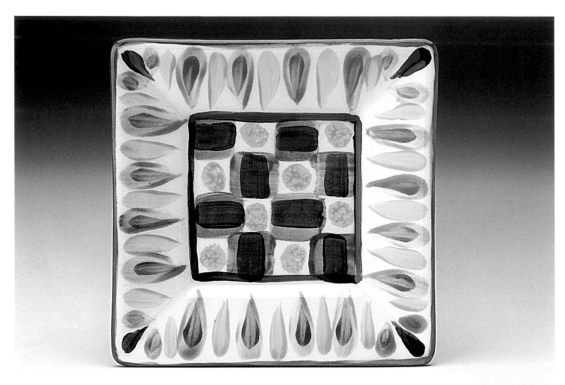

BOWL, DIAMETER 8" (20.3 CM).
I painted this bowl using the same technique as for the square plate, applying each repeating motif with a different type of stroke.

Drybrush is an application method for creating texture or shading, using a brush from which most of the underglaze has been blotted or wiped off.

Dip your brush in the underglaze as usual, but then blot it on a paper towel before applying it to the bisque. Stiff-bristle brushes work best for this technique.

Demonstration: DRYBRUSH

 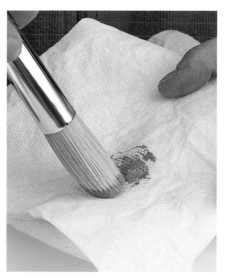 

1 I dip a stiff-bristle brush into the underglaze, picking up color just on the tip.

2 I blot the brush on a paper towel to remove some of the underglaze.

3 I apply the color to my bisqueware piece, establishing visual texture.

SUSAN KRAMER, PLATTER, 14" (35.6 CM) SQUARE.
In this piece the blue background has been made more interesting and varied with the use of drybrush.

Shading

Shading is the process of suggesting volume on a two-dimensional surface by representing shadow and light. In the demonstration that follows I use a smooth-blending technique, in which it's important to apply your colors quickly so that the underglazes remain moist as you work.

Here I use a palette of analogous colors, blending different values of reddish purple to deep cobalt blue to create shading on the body of the eggplant and, for the stem, various values of green. I then add highlights on both areas with a yellow.

There are many other ways to represent light and shadow, of course. For example, you can follow the basic procedure for the eggplant tile shown here but apply the shading and highlighting colors using other techniques, such as drybrush (as described above), or sponging or spattering (described below). Likewise, you don't have to limit yourself to an analogous color palette; you have various possible choices. Look, for instance, at Impressionist paintings to see the broad spectrum of colors artists have used to represent light and shadow. With regard to the eggplant, instead of an analogous darker color for shadow, try a neutralized version of the main hue (in this case, purple) by mixing it with a small amount of its complement (yellow), or try another color altogether, such as turquoise. For light, try any lighter and brighter color—perhaps a bit of orange to highlight the eggplant's purple, or even green. Experiment with your own palette to discover new possibilities, using paint on paper first if you like.

Demonstration: SHADING

1 I draw the eggplant in pencil; the graphite will burn off in the firing.

2 I begin by painting the eggplant with a medium shade of purple, then add a lighter, ruby reddish purple over it, covering about half the area and blending it with the brush into the base coat.

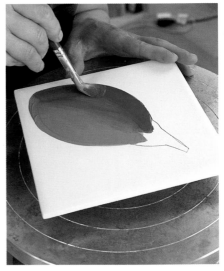

3 I then apply a deep royal purple, starting at the opposite edge and blending it as before. At this point, to exaggerate the shading I add just a tiny amount of a strong cobalt blue to the edge of the deep purple.

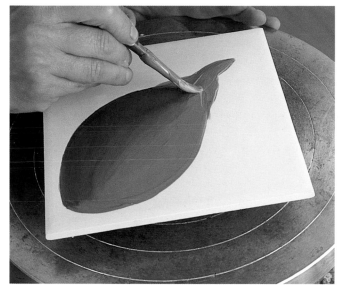 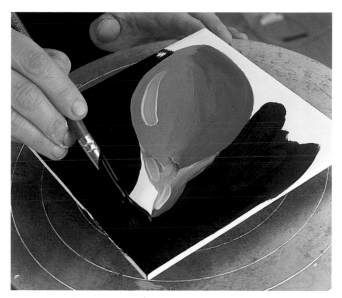

4 I paint the eggplant stem in the same manner, beginning with a medium green and adding a bright green to one side and a dark green on the other side, blending them as I go.

5 Here you can see that I've added yellow highlights to the eggplant and its stem; this contrast helps convey the sense of three-dimensionality even further. In this step I am now applying a very dark underglaze to the background, effectively pushing the eggplant's form forward in space visually.

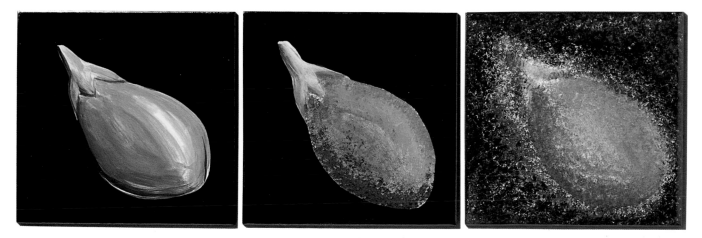

This illustration shows you just a few other options for shading, as well as color choice. In the tile at left, done in a smooth-blending technique, I've used a turquoise blue along the lower part of the eggplant, transitioning to almost (though not quite) analogous reds and purples, with some orange tones for highlights. The center tile combines smooth tonal blending with sponging, while light and shadow on the eggplant tile at right is established mostly with a sponging technique and the use of greens and oranges on the periphery for contrast.

Trailing

Trailing, or slip trailing—sometimes also referred to as piping—is the application of underglaze (or any decorating material) through a plastic squeeze bottle fitted with a narrow nozzle. Trailing is often used for creating linear elements or stippling, as the continuation of the eggplant tile demonstration opposite illustrates. You can also use this technique to outline images for emphasis, or as a decorative element in itself.

Two factors affect the application of underglaze in this manner. The first is the size of the nozzle opening on the squeeze bottle. For relatively fine lines you can buy bottles with metal tips in fine, medium, and bold gauges. Squeeze bottles with plastic cone-shaped nozzles are also available in a variety of sizes; with these you can cut off the tip of the cone to the desired width of the kinds of marks you want to make. There is also a type of squeeze bottle with a nozzle that can be opened and closed by turning it, like that on an Elmer's

Glue bottle. These are a little harder to clean than the others (though all you have to do is open the nozzle and poke a straight pin through it several times, digging out the clogged underglaze), but I like the convenience of not having a separate cap.

The second factor in trailing applications is the viscosity of the underglaze you're using, which will determine how fast it flows from the bottle and how much it will "stand up" on the bisque surface. Applying an underglaze with a thicker viscosity results in a physically dimensional texture, while applying one that is thinner will flatten out, making a wider, shallower line. You may have to water down an underglaze in the squeeze bottle to adjust the viscosity according to your design preference. Many underglaze manufacturers now offer a line packaged in squeeze bottles with relatively fine metal tips; the trade names of these products usually contain the word "dimension" or "dimensional."

Squeeze bottles for trailing techniques. Some have metal tips in various gauges; others have cone-shaped plastic tips that you can trim to suit the width of your marks, while still others are equipped with a one-piece nozzle that you can open and close by turning it.

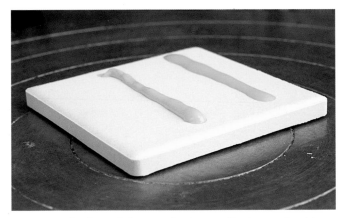

ABOVE: Note the thinned-down underglaze application to the right of the thicker one.

RIGHT: Various trailing applications; at left I've used a narrow-gauge nozzle to make thin lines, and at right am using a wider one for wider lines.

Demonstration: TRAILING

Resuming the eggplant tile demonstration from the preceding section, here I show you how I developed my design further, and how you might want to apply this decorative technique to your own work.

ABOVE: **EGGPLANT TILE, 8" (20.3 CM) SQUARE.**
The eggplant tile after glazing and firing.

After the dark background color of my tile has dried, I apply a scattered spiral motif in a contrasting yellow-green underglaze. Then I add stippling between the spiral pattern with a violet underglaze.

BELOW: **KRISTEN MILLS, THREE BOWLS, DIAMETER 9" (22.9 CM) EACH.**
Note how the artist Kristen Mills has used the trailing technique to create graphically bold linear qualities in her work.

Sponging

Sponges can be used to create many different textural effects; they come in a variety and are widely available and inexpensive, so you can experiment with all of them. Natural sponges, which include those called "elephant ear," "silk," and "wool" sponges, are available in art and craft supply stores and from ceramics suppliers and some hardware stores.

Natural and synthetic sponges and the kinds of marks they make.

There are also synthetic versions of these. Elephant ear and silk sponges are relatively small and dense, whereas wool and other larger natural sponges have a coarse, open structure. Often the texture in a natural sponge varies, so it can be used to create several different effects. Synthetic polyester and cellulose sponges, manufactured mostly as clean-up tools, are generally much more uniform in structure.

As shown below, you apply underglaze—one or more colors—to the sponge with a brush, then dab the sponge directly on the bisqueware. You can also make short brushing strokes with the sponge for a different kind of texture, as illustrated by the black-and-white tiles opposite; here, the sponge marks on the far left and far right were made in this way, whereas the marks in the center were made by applying the sponge directly. To create a multicolor textural effect you can sponge several colors of underglaze, one after another. That's what I did to decorate the rim of my fish platter, opposite.

Demonstration: SPONGING

1 I apply underglaze to my sponge.

2 Then I simply dab it directly on the bisqueware.

3 You can use more than one color at a time on the sponge, as I've done here with orange and yellow.

I made the marks on the far left and far right of these tiles using short, brushing strokes with the sponge; the marks in the center were made by applying the sponge directly.

You can achieve multicolor textural effects by applying several underglazes in succession with a sponge.

FISH PLATTER, LENGTH 23" (58.4 CM).
I used the multicolor sponge technique to decorate the rim of this platter.

Demonstration: SPONGE STAMPING

Some art supply stores offer precut sponge shapes, which are fun. You can also cut your own sponge stamps from regular cellulose sponges. In this demonstration I'm using two different sponge stamps, along with some brushwork, to decorate a liquid-soap dispenser.

1 Cellulose sponge stamps in two different shapes.

2 I apply a light blue underglaze on the surface of my stamp using a brush.

3 I carefully press the underglaze-coated surface of the sponge against the side of my bisque piece at regular intervals, coating the sponge with more color before each application to the piece.

4 Here I'm applying a light purple underglaze between the sponged areas.

5 Once the underglazes have dried to the touch, I use the star-shaped sponge stamp to add another design element, this time with a dark blue.

6 The finished soap dispenser after glazing and firing.

LILAC BOUQUET BOWL, DIAMETER 13¹/₂" (34.3 CM), AND PITCHER, HEIGHT 9¹/₂" (24.1 CM).
Here, I rendered the lilac flowers using the sponging technique.

LEFT: **HYDRANGEA VASE, HEIGHT 11" (27.9 CM).**   RIGHT: **LEMON VASE, HEIGHT 9" (22.9 CM).**
With sponging I created texture in the background areas of these two vases.

Masking

Masking is the process of covering a selected part or parts of your bisque piece to protect areas where you want to maintain the white background or an underlying color. Once the mask is in place, you apply underglazes, then remove the mask before proceeding. There's no need to wait for the underglaze to dry completely first; it dries to the touch very quickly, and that's sufficient. In fact, it's better to remove masking while underglaze is still moist, because if it dries completely it can flake at the edges when you pull up the mask.

The essential thing about masking is that it is removable. This allows you to create backgrounds or shapes in a loose, spontaneous manner, or use techniques such as sponging or spattering, while maintaining crisp edges in the masked area.

As you'll see, there are many materials that can be used as masks. Among the most obvious is masking tape, which is excellent for making straight lines, stripes, and grids. It comes in various widths and degrees of tackiness. Because generally you won't be leaving masking tape on your piece for long periods of time, you can use a cheap hardware-store brand for most decorating projects. However, if you're working on a complex piece over the course of several days, it's worth buying an artist's-grade masking tape, as it won't leave a gummy residue on the bisque surface.

Demonstration: MASKING

1 Apply masking tape in the desired pattern. Make sure the edges of the tape are smoothed over the curves of the piece.

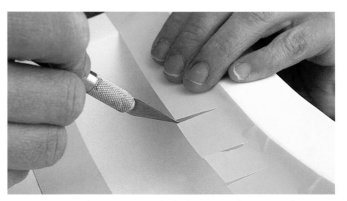

2 To accommodate curves, make little cuts in the tape with a craft knife.

3 After making your cuts in the tape, smooth it down.

4 Then cover the resulting gaps with small pieces of tape.

5 Now you can apply underglazes using any technique you choose, and then remove the tape. Your stripes, lines, or grid can also be embellished using freehand painting or any other technique.

6 Masking tape can also be cut with a craft knife or torn after it has been applied to the bisque to create interesting edges.

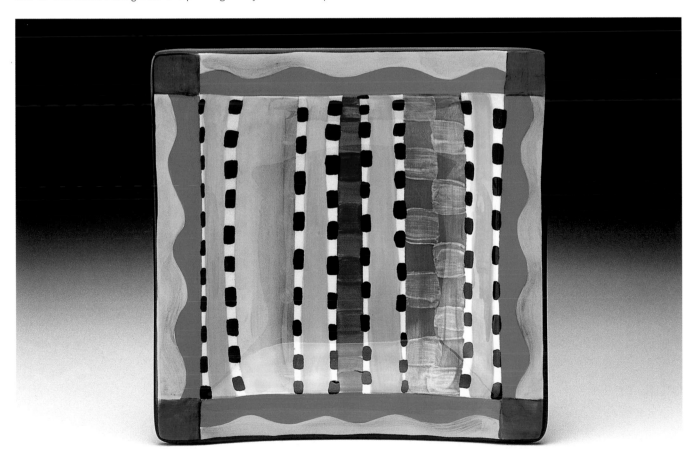

BOWL, 9" (22.9 CM) SQUARE.
To create the wavy border, I cut areas of the masking tape with a craft knife.

Adhesive paper, such as frisket paper or contact paper, can be used for masking out areas of a design or image. To mask with adhesive paper, draw your shape on the nonadhesive side (the shiny side) using a fine-point permanent marker. Cut it out, peel off the back, and adhere it to the bisque surface, smoothing down the edges. For complex shapes it may be easier to cut out parts in adhesive paper and assemble them into the desired arrangement on the piece. Following the same procedure as with the masking tape, apply underglazes, remove the masks, and proceed with your design.

Any peel-and-stick paper or plastic can be used for masking. In stationery or office supply stores you can find adhesive labels in many different shapes and sizes—color-coding dots, Cheerio-shaped stickers used for reinforcing loose-leaf paper, stars, seals, alphabets and numbers used for signs and posters, animal motifs, flowers—almost anything imaginable. These are inexpensive, widely available, and lots of fun!

Perforated papers such as paper doilies and Japanese or Thai lace papers can serve as masks as well. Used in conjunction with solid masks or stenciling, they let you create textural effects to use as backgrounds or other design elements.

TOP: **FRUIT AND VEGETABLE TILES, 8" (20.3 CM) SQUARE EACH.**
I masked off the fruit and vegetable shapes with contact paper. I painted the backgrounds, removed the masks, then rendered the fruits and vegetables.

ABOVE: Stickers are fun masking tools; that's what I used to decorate these tiles.

RIGHT: Here I used lace papers in three different patterns as masks.

Demonstration: MULTIPLE MASKING

Using several different masking materials on one piece, you can create complex and interesting patterns and images. In the following demonstration I use masking tape, lace paper, contact paper, round stickers (used for price tags), and loose-leaf-paper reinforcers.

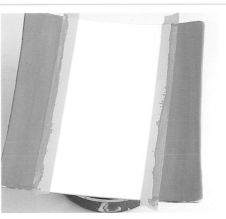

1 I first masked off the center area of my bisque platter with masking tape and painted the two side areas light purple. Here I let this base coat dry somewhat longer than I might otherwise so that the lace paper I apply in the next step won't stick to it.

2 Using a piece of lace paper as a mask, I apply a darker purple over it.

3 After letting this layer dry—though not completely—I remove the lace paper mask.

4 I then remove the tape.

5 Here I'm applying seed-pod shapes, which I cut out of contact paper; after that I added round stickers in an allover pattern.

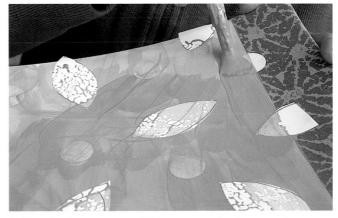

6 Next, I paint two coats of light green underglaze over the center section of the platter.

7 When this base coat was dry to the touch, I sponge-stenciled a compound leaf motif in two shades of green.

8 Here I'm lifting the stencil from the lighter green leaves. (For more on this technique, see the section on stenciling, page 71.)

9 I peel off the contact paper masks and round stickers using a craft knife.

10 Next, I apply loose-leaf-paper reinforcers to the exposed seed-pod shapes.

11 I paint those areas in rose underglaze.

12 When this color is dry to the touch, I remove the stickers.

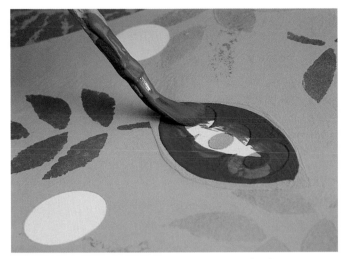

13 I paint over these areas with a transparent violet, leaving most of the outer edges of the shapes their original rose color.

14 The round areas are painted in rose. After adding some more details (see the finished piece), I then applied a clear glaze in preparation for firing.

**PLATE, 11"
(27.9 CM) SQUARE.**
The finished,
fired piece.

Masking Fluid

Masking fluid, sometimes called frisket, is liquid latex, applied with a brush and impervious to moisture when dry. It becomes stretchy and rubberlike and is easily removed. Masking fluid made for watercolor painting, found in art supply stores, can be used, but it's of a thin consistency and is a little tricky to remove from bisqueware unless you apply a couple of coats. Some ceramics suppliers offer liquid latex formulated especially for use on bisqueware. Duncan makes a product called Mask 'n Peel, which has a nice thick, smooth consistency. Any of the above will work. Note: After using brushes with masking fluid, wash them thoroughly in water.

I use masking fluid in the same way I'd use masking tape, but in areas where I need a fluid application such as the rim of a plate, as shown here. (The demonstration for this piece continues on page 67.)

Demonstration: MASKING FLUID

1 I apply the masking fluid around the rim of my plate with a brush and let it dry completely.

3 Then I paint the now exposed area.

2 After painting my design in the center of the plate, I remove the masking fluid from the rim; you simply peel it off.

This term comes from the Italian *graffiare*, which means to scratch, and refers to the technique of scratching a line or texture into the surface of something as a means of decorating it. In the making of ceramics it means scratching into the surface of wet clay, producing both physical and visual texture. In decorating premade bisqueware, we use sgraffito to scratch through a layer of underglaze to reveal the white bisque underneath or a previously applied coat of underglaze. *Note: If you're using a base coat of underglaze, make sure that it's completely dry before applying the subsequent color, and use sgraffito technique when this second coat is still moist (half-dry).*

There are many different sgraffito tools available at ceramics supply stores, but any pointed instrument can be used. Different tools will result in different line qualities. I usually use a knitting needle, as its somewhat rounded point gives the line a smooth and open quality. A pen or pencil works just as well, and the ink or graphite will burn out in the kiln and won't show up after firing. A sharp pointed instrument will make a finer line than a knitting needle or ballpoint pen. Experiment with different tools to discover the variety of marks you can make.

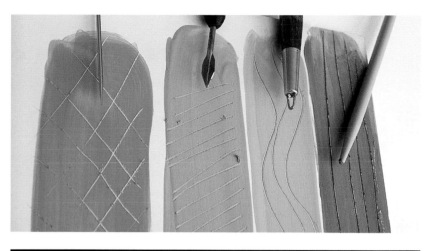

TOP: Here are just a few tools you can use in the sgraffito technique. Experiment with different ones to discover the variety of marks you can make.

ABOVE: **KRISTEN MILLS, TWO SMALL TRAYS, 7 × 4¹/₂" (17.8 × 11.4 CM) EACH.** LEFT: **LITTLE CONDIMENT DISHES, 3" (7.6 CM) SQUARE EACH.** Examples of how sgraffito can be used as a decorative technique to reveal the white bisque underneath or a previously applied coat of underglaze color.

Demonstration: LINEAR SGRAFFITO

Sgraffito can be used simply to make lines, to outline or emphasize your underglaze decoration, as in the following plate demonstration.

1 Using a mechanical pencil, I draw the veins on the leaves while the underglaze color is still a little damp.

2 Here I'm applying underglaze to the plate's rim, where I've planned to use more sgraffito decoration.

3 Adding the sgraffito motif while the underglaze is still damp. The dark pencil marks will burn off during firing, as you can see in the finished piece.

LEAF PLATE, DIAMETER 10" (25.4 CM).

Demonstration: TEXTURAL SGRAFFITO

You can also do cross-hatching or other close-together mark making to create areas of texture, as in the background of this artichoke plate. (This is a continuation of the sequence shown on page 64.)

1 For this piece, to create the background around my artichoke design, I first brush on several colors of underglaze, overlapping them loosely.

2 When these colors dry just to the touch—that is, they remain somewhat damp—I apply my sgraffito tool to create a texture over the whole background area.

3 I apply more color by brushing lightly over the top surfaces of the sgraffito marks.

ARTICHOKE PLATE, DIAMETER 10" (25.4 CM).
The glazed and fired plate. Note that I added some sgraffito outlines around the artichoke leaves; this, along with the background texture, helps create the illusion of depth.

Spattering

Here I am using a toothbrush to spatter green underglaze over a layer of spattered yellow.

Spattering is best done with a stiff-bristled brush or a toothbrush. Apply underglaze—thinned a little with water if necessary—with a paintbrush to the tips of the toothbrush bristles (you can dip the toothbrush in the underglaze, but applying it with a brush gives you more control). Run your thumb over the toothbrush while holding it close to the bisque surface. You can layer several colors in this manner to create a texture, as I'm doing here.

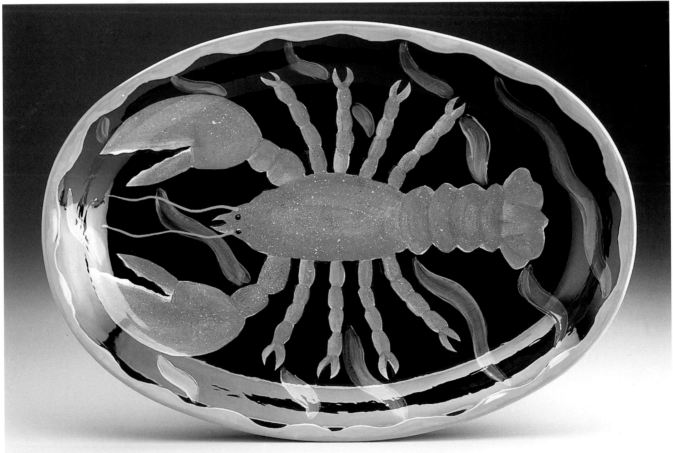

LOBSTER PLATTER, 13 × 19" (33 × 48.3 см).
I spattered white and black underglazes to add a speckled look over the lobster's red body before painting in the black background.

Stamping is a great way to create a consistent repeated image. Commercially made stamps are available in a vast variety of shapes and sizes from almost any store that sells art and craft materials. With linoleum-cutting tools you can also carve your own from flexible rubber made for this purpose; you'll find this material at craft supply stores, and in the printmaking department at art supply stores. If you are carving your own, the areas *not* to be printed are hollowed out of the stamp so that the motif stands out from the background—that is, in relief—and is the part that will receive underglaze color. A technical note: Stamps of any size can be used on a flat surface, but on a curved surface, smaller ones work better.

Before stamping underglaze colors on a bisqueware piece, let the base coat dry completely (or nearly so); otherwise the stamp will lift or disturb the undercoat.

ABOVE: **SAMPLER PLATE WITH STAMP MOTIFS, 12" (30.5 CM) SQUARE.** Here I used a combination of commercial and handmade stamps.

LEFT: **STAMPED FISH PLATTER, 11 × 15"** (27.9 × 38.1 CM). For this platter I used commercially made stamps (along with some spattering and, at right, a lace-paper mask).

Demonstration: STAMPING

In this demonstration I use three different stamps I made myself, carved out of a flexible rubber material.

1 I've prepared this square plate with a light-value beige underglaze in the center and a darker one on the sides; both base coats are dry at this point. With a brush I apply a black underglaze to the raised surfaces—those in relief—of my stamp.

2 I then press the underglaze-coated side of the stamp to the center of my bisqueware piece.

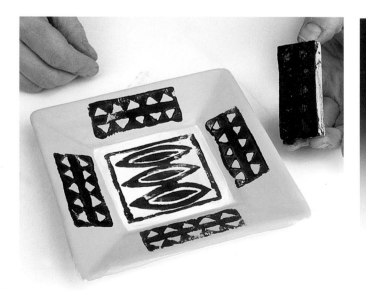

3 Here's the result of the first stamp application in the center of the plate, and a second one in a different pattern applied to its four raised rims.

PLATE, 6" (15.2 CM) SQUARE.
Working as before, I stamped a third motif onto the four corners of the plate, as you can see here in the glazed and fired finish.

Stenciling is sort of like masking in reverse. Essentially, you're masking out the background while you paint the figure—"figure" here meaning the subject of (or objects in) the composition of the piece you're decorating, as distinguished from the background, or "ground," of your design.

Stenciling lends itself well to creating pattern. It's also a good way to make intricate images that would be very difficult or time consuming to paint directly. Like masking, stenciling allows you to maintain crisp edges while applying underglazes in a loose, spontaneous manner. I find it exciting to use masking techniques in combination with stenciling to achieve anything from subtle textural effects to complex, collagelike imagery. (Refer to the multiple-masking demonstration on pages 61–63 to see what I mean.)

Unlike masking materials used for decorating ceramics, most commercially available stencils don't have an adhesive backing, which can make using them on a vertical or curved surface tricky. There are, however, adhesive-backed stencils made especially for decorating bisqueware, and these are available from some ceramics suppliers. You can also cut your own stencils from frisket paper or contact paper, or hold stencils in place with masking tape.

Once a stencil is in position, you can use a stencil brush—a round brush with the bristles forming a flat, blunt end—or even a sponge, to apply underglaze. I find that for nonadhesive stencils a sponge application works best, as this method gives you a great deal of control over the amount of underglaze applied and helps avoid color running under the stencil.

BELOW: Here I've used a homemade stencil to paint a lemon. I applied the first coat of yellow to define its shape, then sponged a slightly darker shade of yellow along the bottom of the fruit to give it dimension.

ABOVE AND RIGHT: Here I'm using a commercial stencil to add a motif to a plate decorated with washes of underglaze. *In this case any previous underglaze application must be completely dry before you stencil over it.*

Demonstration: STENCILING

1 Here I'm using commercial adhesive-backed stencils, which are useful when you're working on a vertical surface.

2 I apply the underglaze with a brush.

3 When the color is dry to the touch (still moist), I simply peel off the stencils.

Demonstration: COMBINING SPONGING AND STENCILING

To decorate this large rectangular platter, I combine sponging and stenciling techniques (along with a little masking) to create a variegated foliage design.

1 I prepared the platter by dividing it into two sections with a strip of masking tape. I painted a base coat of light green underglaze on the smaller section and a base coat of orange with a variegated sponged pattern on the larger section.

2 On the larger section of the platter, using homemade stencils and a sponge, I create the maple leaves with several reds and oranges and a bit of yellow-green. For the compound leaves in this area (see next step) I used several greens.

3 I then sponged a slightly darker green gradation over the green base coat on the smaller section of the platter and stencil another leaf pattern, again using several different greens.

4 When the underglazes are dry just to the touch, I remove the masking tape between the two sections. Now I paint the exposed stripe with plum and violet underglazes.

FOLIAGE SUSHI PLATTER, 11 × 15" (28 × 38 см).
Here is the finished piece after glazing and firing.

Spritzing and Blotting

This technique is comparable to "lifting" in watercolor painting, in that you wet parts of an area already painted, and then remove color from that area. The basic technique is to apply your underglaze to the bisqueware and let it dry until it is just slightly damp. Using a spray bottle, gently spritz a little water onto the ware and let it settle for a few seconds. Then with a paper towel or soft tissue, blot the surface carefully.

The underglaze will lift off where the water droplets fell, and remain intact elsewhere. You can use this technique between several layers of underglaze, creating a complex mottling effect. The variability of the spray droplets, from a coarse squirt to a fine mist, gives you a range of possible textures. For more control you can apply water using an eye dropper and proceed with the blotting as described here.

Demonstration: SPRITZING AND BLOTTING

1 I spritzed some water on this tile while the underglaze was still slightly damp.

2 After letting the water settle briefly, I gently blot the tile with a paper towel.

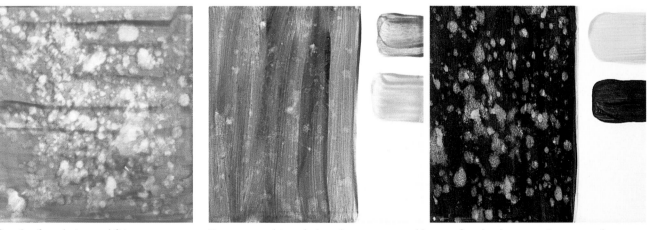

3 The tile after glazing and firing.

You can use this technique between several layers of underglaze, creating a complex mottling effect, as here.

With transfer techniques you apply underglaze to a surface, then transfer it to the bisque. While stamping and sponging fall into this category, here are a few more unusual methods.

Acetate

Acetate is a transparent film used in graphic arts to make overlays. On regular acetate, a water-based medium, including underglaze, will repel the surface and form little beads. There's also a kind of acetate treated especially for use with watermedia, on which the application of underglaze will remain intact; this is the type I used for the demonstrations below. *Note:* If you're layering one underglaze color over another, make sure the first layer is completely dry before transferring a second color over it; otherwise the acetate may remove pieces of the base coat.

Demonstration: ACETATE TRANSFER

1 With a brush I apply underglaze to the acetate.

2 While the underglaze is still wet I press the acetate, face down, onto the bisqueware just for a moment.

3 I remove the acetate. Note the textural effects this technique produces.

Demonstration: ACETATE TRANSFER WITH FINGER PAINTING

1 Here I finger paint over the underglaze brushed on the acetate. You can also alter it otherwise.

2 The underglaze as it looks after I transfer it to the bisque piece.

FISH TRANSFER PLATE, DIAMETER 12" (30.5 CM).
Here I used acetate transfers over my base-coat colors to create the texture in the center of the plate, and to create the fish—with some finger painting on the acetate—around the rim. Remember: In this technique, when transferring underglaze color over a base coat, make sure the latter is completely dry first.

UTENSIL HOLDER WITH LIZARD, HEIGHT 6¹/₂" (16.5 CM).
Another example of transferred color layered over underlying colors, with some finger-painted detail in the underglaze transfer.

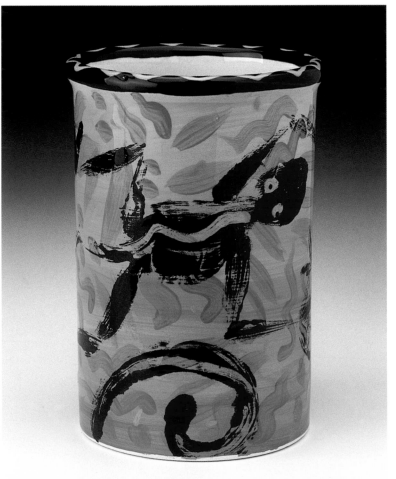

Wax Paper

Underglaze, when applied to wax paper, beads up, much as it would on untreated acetate. Besides painting underglaze on a flat sheet of wax paper, another thing you can do with this surface that's not possible with acetate is to scrunch it up before applying the underglaze. This will give you an interesting textural variation.

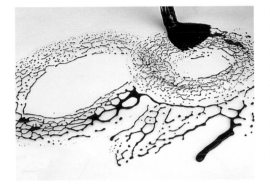

LEFT: Note how underglaze beads up when I apply it to wax paper.

BELOW LEFT: The tile at left shows a black-on-white wax paper transfer; the one at right is a color example.

BELOW: Here I crumpled wax paper before applying underglaze to it.

"FANTASY FLOWERS" PLATTER, 8 × 15" (20.3 × 38.1 CM).
After masking off the orange petal-like shapes beforehand, I used a wax paper transfer to apply color over the base coat to the center background area of this platter.

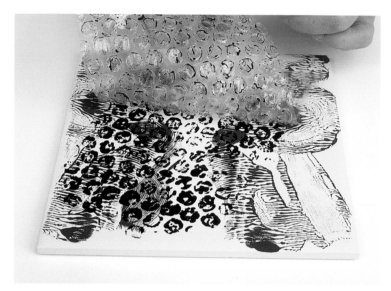

Bubblewrap

Bubblewrap, too, offers some good decorative options; experiment with different sizes and types of bubblewrap to create interesting textures.

LEFT: Try different kinds of bubblewrap for a variety of effects. Here I've layered a bubblewrap transfer over an acetate transfer.

BELOW: **"2 OF HEARTS" PLATE, 12" (30.5 CM) SQUARE.** I used the transfer technique with bubblewrap to add texture to the hearts on this plate.

Paper Towel

Still another transfer method involves the use of a paper towel. It's a little different from the preceding ones, in that the paper towel is a permeable material.

Demonstration: PAPER TOWEL TRANSFER

1 I apply my underglaze image to the paper towel.

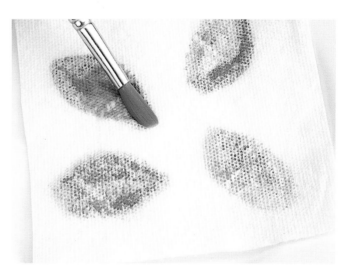

2 I place the image face down on the bisque surface, and then gently wet the back of the paper towel with water using a soft, clean brush; a sponge works well here too.

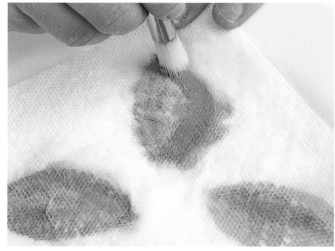

3 The image will distort a little from the water. You can control this to some extent by the amount of water you use and the amount of pressure you apply.

4 I remove the paper towel showing the leaf motif. I then enhanced the leaves and background with underglaze pencils. The finished, glazed and fired plate is shown on page 80.

Underglaze Pencils

Underglaze pencils are like colored pencils or soft pastels and are particularly appealing to novice ceramics painters and children because they're such an easy, direct medium to handle.

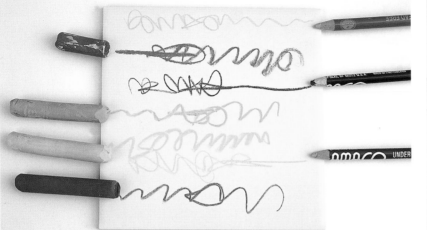

ABOVE, LEFT AND RIGHT: In the tile samples shown here I used underglaze pencils directly on a white bisque surface. The example at left shows you what they look like before glazing and firing, while the one at right, afterward.

RIGHT: **LEAF PLATE, DIAMETER 10" (25.4 CM).**
Underglaze pencils can be used interestingly over a base coat of underglaze, as in this plate. I created the leaf motif here using the paper towel transfer technique described on the preceding page.

Painted faux marble finishes, very popular as decorative motifs, are typically applied to woodwork, doors, pillars, or table-tops, where actual marble might be used. Ceramic tiles would fit into this tradition very well. It's fun, however, to take this technique out of the architectural realm and apply it to dinnerware and other ceramic home furnishings, and it translates well to the use of underglazes.

FAUX MARBLE CANDLESTICKS, HEIGHT 6" (15.2 CM).
A pair of candlesticks decorated with the marbling technique.

FAUX MARBLE LAMP, HEIGHT 22" (55.9 CM).
After glazing and firing this lamp base, I applied accents with gold leaf and created the faux marble shade with acrylic paints.

Demonstration: MARBLING—DARK VEINS ON LIGHT GROUND

In this demonstration I show how to paint a coral-colored faux marble; the same sequence of steps can be used to make any other color as well.

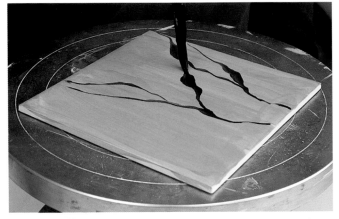

1 First I applied two coats of my base underglaze color, a coral hue. Next, using a black underglaze, I paint the veins with slow, uneven strokes. Each layer of color need only be dry to the touch before you apply another one.

2 While the black is still wet, I brush over it with a watered-down white underglaze (an off-white would work here too), allowing my brushstrokes to distort the black veins. The amount of water you add to the underglaze for this step should give you a mixture that's just thin enough to flow freely—perhaps one part water to one part color, or one-third water to two-thirds color; there's no exact formula.

3 While the previous application remains damp, I add more black veins sparingly to suggest depth and a translucent quality.

4 Now I selectively apply an underglaze wash (underglaze thinned with water) of the base color—coral, in this case—and a bit of ochre, distorting some, but not all, of the veining.

5 If you wish, you can apply, selectively, another wash of white or off-white while the previous coat is damp, as I'm doing here. This adds a little more visual depth and contrast.

Demonstration: MARBLING—LIGHT VEINS ON DARK GROUND

In the following demonstration I use a slightly different technique to create a greenish black marble with white and ochre veins.

1 First I paint a tile with two coats of deep green underglaze; then, when this is dry, I brush on a watered-down black underglaze (thinned just enough to be somewhat transparent), rotating my brush in a circular motion. The black will become more translucent when glazed and fired so you'll be able to see the green underneath it.

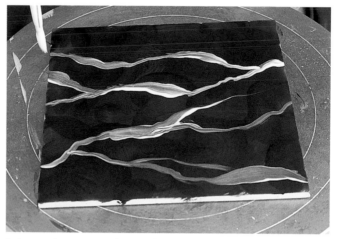

2 I paint the veins in white underglaze; if you have both translucent and opaque white underglazes, use the two of them, as they will add more depth to the fired piece.

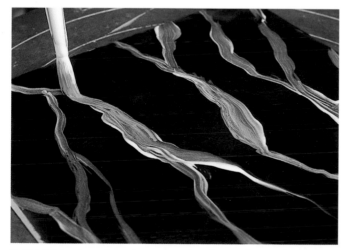

3 I highlight the veins selectively with a deep yellow underglaze; an ochre would also work well here.

RIGHT: Here are the glazed and fired results of the two demonstration tiles, plus two others.

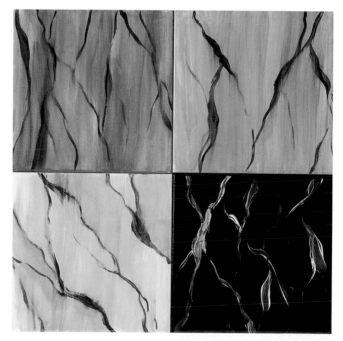

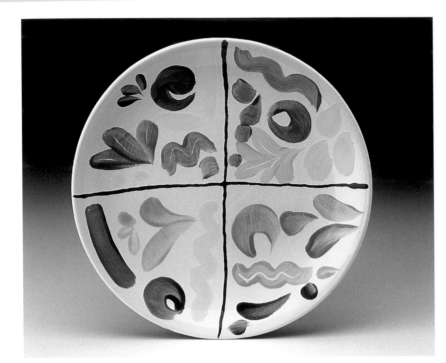

Majolica test plate. I used, clockwise from top left, underglaze decorating colors; underglazes modified with majolica glaze; matte colored glazes; and gloss colored glazes.

SO FAR I'VE SHOWN YOU how to decorate white bisqueware by painting pieces with colored underglazes, then coat them with a clear glaze before the final firing in the kiln. Majolica (pronounced either with a hard *j* or, as in the original Italian, *maiolica*, with a *y* sound) is a technique in which the blank bisqueware piece is coated first with an opaque white glaze, called majolica glaze, then decorated using any of the materials described below. It's best if the majolica glaze is dry before you proceed.

Once the piece is decorated, no further glazing is required before firing. This is called an "in glaze," as opposed to "underglaze," technique, because during the firing process the colors melt into the white glaze, becoming structurally integrated with it. By contrast, with the underglaze technique, the colors remain literally under the clear glaze.

MAJOLICA BOWL, DIAMETER 5" (12.7 CM).

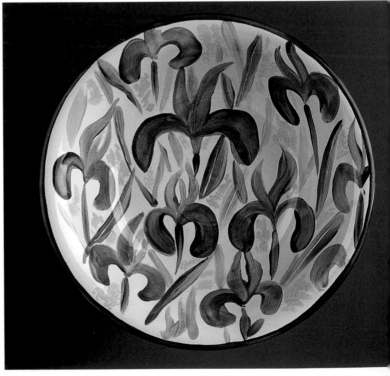

IRIS BOWL, DIAMETER 8" (20.3 CM).

Most manufacturers of underglazes also offer a majolica glaze with compatible majolica decorating colors. Though these specially formulated colors are dependable and consistent, they are but one of several different possibilities. You can make any of your underglazes into majolica decorating colors by adding a bit of the white majolica glaze, say about one part glaze to three or four parts underglaze. You may want to make a test tile of the colors you intend to use on the majolica glaze before using them on bisqueware. Colored glazes, both gloss and matte (discussed in chapter 4), can be used as majolica colors. In my tests, I've found that the different brands of glazes and underglazes are compatible, but you may want to do your own test pieces to be sure. The test piece on the opposite page illustrates four different approaches to majolica technique: underglaze decorating colors, underglazes modified with majolica glaze, matte colored glazes, and gloss colored glazes.

When applying the majolica glaze, it's important to get a smooth, even surface. If you're dipping your piece in the glaze, this is usually not an issue. However, if you're brushing on the glaze, make sure it is thinned enough with water—to the consistency of heavy cream—so as not to leave evident brushstrokes. If there are irregularities in the surface of the glaze, the subsequent decoration will pick it up.

Most of the techniques covered in this chapter are applicable to the majolica method of decoration. The main differences in the fired results are that the edges of your brushstrokes, sponge marks, etc., will blur as the color melts into the glaze, so the overall look is softer than that of underglaze; and the fired colors will not be as intense, as they are diluted by the white glaze underneath.

If you're adding sgraffito decoration, you need to use a light pressure with your sgraffito tool so that you scratch through the layer of color only, and not through the white glaze underneath. Be sure the glaze is very dry before decorating over it. This makes it easier to apply the color without lifting the glaze, especially if you're using adhesive masking materials, transfer techniques, or stamping.

The objects shown on these two pages are all examples of majolica technique.

TOP: **GEORGANNA (JANNO) GAY, "ITALIAN PLUM" OVAL PLATTER,** 13 × 16" (33 × 40.6 CM).

ABOVE: **GEORGANNA (JANNO) GAY, "SUMMER FRUIT" MUGS, HEIGHT 4"** (10.2 CM) EACH.

4

Colored Glazes and Postfiring Applications: An Overview

FOR THOSE OF YOU who feel you're ready to move to the next level of ceramics decoration, I present in this chapter a rather broad overview of colored glazes and a glimpse at just a few of the ways they can be used. Because colored glazes differ significantly from underglazes in many respects and come in such variety, it would be impossible in the space of this book for me to discuss them in great depth. However, I hope this brief introduction will pique your interest.

Also included in this chapter are a few materials and techniques that can be used on ceramic wares that have already been fired and are intended as purely decorative objects.

If nothing else, let the information and accompanying illustrations offered here inspire you to pursue more advanced creative options!

COLORED GLAZES

DECORATING WITH colored glazes can be exciting and challenging, both from an aesthetic point of view and a technical one. Colored glazes are different from underglazes, with many more variables to consider; like underglazes, they are available in an almost endless variety of colors, but they also offer numerous surface qualities: glossy, satin matte, or matte; transparent, semitransparent, opaque, or semi-opaque; ones that simulate the look of gunmetal or bronze; some that produce very textured surfaces; and others that result in effects such as crackling or mottling. (All such qualities are indicated on manufacturers' labels.) Certain specialty glazes are inappropriate for dinnerware, but can be very exciting to use on decorative pieces.

The main difference between colored glazes and underglazes is that colored glazes melt and fuse into glass during the firing process (as do clear glazes, as discussed in chapter 1), forming the glassy surface that makes the bisqueware to which they're applied relatively impermeable to liquids, and functional. But colored glazes contain colorants and other modifiers, allowing you to apply color and the glassy surface in one step.

So, why not just use colored glazes all the time, one step instead of two? The answer is that the behavior of colored glazes during the firing process differs significantly from that of underglazes. Also, they must be handled and applied differently. For one thing, a colored glaze must cover, in an even layer, the entire surface of the piece (except on the foot where it touches the kiln shelf). Applying a colored glaze is much more like putting an even layer of icing on a cake than it is like painting. For another thing, often a colored glaze in its raw state bears little or no resemblance to its fired result, as you can see in the illustration below.

Basic Composition and Properties

Since I'm discussing only commercially made colored glazes, I won't go into chemical complexities here. However, a fundamental understanding of their composition and behavior is useful in choosing the types you might wish to use for given projects.

Glazes are basically glass, which is mostly silica, modified to meet the requirements of ceramics. A glaze must adhere to the surface of the bisque in its raw state and during firing (and of course after firing). In the high temperatures of the kiln the glaze melts on the surface of the bisqueware and becomes a thick, sticky, honeylike substance. Alumina is added to the silica to prevent the glaze from running down the side of the piece and to keep it relatively viscous in its melted state. The other basic requirement is that the glaze actually melt at a

Raw colored glazes on their corresponding fired samples.

specified kiln temperature. Silica on its own would require much hotter temperatures to melt, but there are various chemicals, called *fluxes,* that can be added to reduce the melting temperature. A strong flux will produce a runny glaze (one that may drip or pool during firing), whereas a less strong flux will produce a stiffer glaze, one that moves very little during firing. The particular fluxes added to a glaze usually contribute to other characteristics as well, such as color, surface quality, and texture.

Usually it's important to apply colored glazes evenly to the surface of your bisque piece, and much more thickly than you would with underglazes. The application should be as smooth as possible, without obvious brushstroke marks or drips. Brushing on a colored glaze is technically just like brushing on a clear glaze as described in chapter 1. The consistency of the glaze should be about like that of heavy cream. Good, even coverage usually involves three coats, letting each dry between applications. The process can be very time consuming, depending on how many colors you use on one piece, but the results are unlike anything you could achieve using underglazes. The thickness of the glaze application affects the fired result, often dramatically. A too-thin application will usually result in a dry, rough surface, when the glaze is supposed to give you a smooth and glossy or satin matte finish. On the other hand, a too-thick application can cause the glaze to "crawl," or bead up on itself in places, leaving areas of exposed bisque surface, as illustrated above at right. With some glazes you may want to experiment with this range of characteristics by deliberately applying them thick in some areas and thin in others.

Safety in Handling Glazes

It's important to read the information on the labels of glaze containers about safe handling and use of the products. There are usually four safety categories:

- *Nontoxic:* This means that the glaze contains no toxic materials, and no particular precautions need be taken with them. If accidentally ingested in a small quantity, such glazes are usually harmless. They can be used on dinnerware without poisoning your food.
- *Nontoxic but inappropriate for use on dinnerware:* The glaze contains nontoxic materials and is therefore safe to handle without precautions, but results in a surface that's undesirable for food service. Such products include very matte glazes, textured glazes, and also crackle glazes, the latter of which are not completely impervious to liquids.
- *Dinnerware safe when fired to specified temperature:* The glaze contains a small amount of lead (or other hazardous material) but is dinnerware safe when fired as specified. This means that when handling the raw glaze you must take precautions, but that after

TOP: In these four little bowls, note that the amber glaze ran and pooled during firing, as did the two green glazes, though to a lesser extent; the brown glaze didn't run at all.

ABOVE: An example of glaze "crawling."

firing (as on dinnerware), it will not poison your food. Firing chemically binds the lead in this type of glaze, preventing it from leaching out.

- *Toxic and not dinnerware safe:* This category includes many specialized types, such as crystal and metallic glazes. These are to be handled with caution and used only on surfaces that do not come into contact with food. Lamps, vases, bathroom accessories, clocks, boxes, decorative platters, and tiles are among the many kinds of pieces on which these glazes can be used safely.

Most manufacturers' catalogs list non-toxic glazes separately from those that contain toxic materials, which are usually described as "professional," "specialty," or "art" glazes. Safety information is always included in the catalog, but if you want more details, ask for a Material Safety Data Sheet (MSDS); ceramics materials manufacturers are required to provide MSDSs for all of their products upon request.

The following precautions should be taken with any glaze containing lead or other toxic materials: Put newspaper down under your glazing area. When you're finished working, fold the newspaper carefully to contain all glaze residue and discard it in a container that's not accessible to children or animals. Wear an apron or clothes designated for studio use only. Wash your hands after glazing. Do not eat or smoke while glazing.

Testing Colored Glazes

As with underglazes, it's very useful to make fired samples of each colored glaze you intend to use so that you can determine its color and surface characteristics, translucency or opacity, thickness parameters (how the fired results vary with the thickness of application), and how much it is subject to running or pooling during firing. (Note: Contemporary ceramics studios generally don't offer colored glazes, but you could prepare glaze tests at home and have a studio fire them if you don't have your own kiln; call ahead about firing policy.) The following procedure will give you all of this information.

Demonstration: TESTING COLORED GLAZES

1 Using a small, steep-sided bowl, mark the bottom of the piece with underglaze or underglaze pencil with the name or code of the glaze to be tested.

2 Brush a stripe of black underglaze across the interior of the bowl.

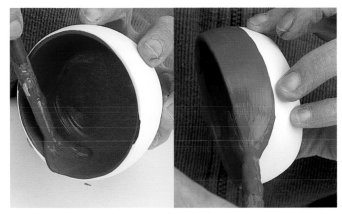

3 When the underglaze is completely dry, brush one even coat of colored glaze over the interior of the bowl and partway down its side.

4 When the first coat of colored glaze is completely dry, brush a second coat over three-quarters of the area covered by the first coat, perpendicular to the underglaze stripe.

5 When the second coat of colored glaze is dry, apply a third coat to half of the bowl.

6 When the third coat of colored glaze is dry, apply a fourth coat to one-quarter of the bowl.

After firing, note how the thickness of the application affects color, surface quality, opacity, and tendency to run or pool. Some of these qualities will vary only slightly with thickness of application, while others may be more dramatic. Sometimes the differences can be very subtle.

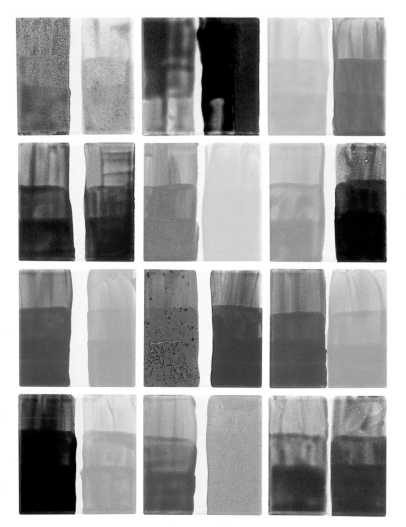

Fired test tiles showing one, two, and three coats of colored glazes.

Another variable you can test is firing temperature. If your normal firing temperature is cone 05 (as assumed here), you may find it useful to test all your glazes at cone 06 and 04, or even at a wider temperature range. Prepare glaze tests as described above, either as small bowls or as tiles, making a set for each temperature variable, and clearly mark the cone number on the bottom of the test pieces with an underglaze pencil. Fire each set of tests to the indicated cone number. This will give you an idea about each glaze's temperature range; some will vary dramatically, and some very little. This is easily done if you have a small test kiln, or even a regular kiln loaded only with your glaze tests. While using the latter may not be the most efficient use of electricity, you can judge for yourself if the expenditure is worth the information to be gained. If you become very involved with colored glazes, a test kiln may be a good investment. (See "Kilns" in the appendices.)

Layering Colored Glazes

Because colored glazes react with one another chemically during the firing process, layering one over another can produce interesting and often unexpected results. Indeed, the possibilities are endless and, in complexity, go beyond what you can accomplish by layering underglazes, the object of which is to mix or modify color.

There are many ways you can explore these effects; some of mine are shown here. In doing your own tests, what's important is that you make accurate notes as to which glazes you use and the order in which you apply them. You can have two quite different results by reversing the layering order of the same two glazes.

You can simplify this process by testing one, two, and three coats of glaze, dividing the bowl into thirds instead of quarters. Another approach is to use small tiles, which will give you all the necessary information except how much the glaze will run or pool when applied to a vertical surface. Used on their own, most commercial glazes won't run or pool significantly, but when one color or type of colored glaze is layered over another the combination may produce a runny effect even if neither glaze is particularly soft on its own. Do a separate set of tests for layering (see below).

LEFT: I applied two coats of each of four colored glazes of different types (glossy, matte, specialty, etc.), then did the same with four more in the opposite direction. This is a quick way to test a lot of combinations.

ABOVE: In the top row of tiles I layered one glaze over another; in the bottom row I reversed the order. Some results are dramatic, others very subtle.

In this example I tested five different gloss glazes over five differ-ent matte glazes. I brushed two coats of each matte glaze onto the interior of the bowl in concentric circles, then applied two coats of each gloss glaze in pie-shape wedges up to the rim of the bowl. This gives me additional information as to how the glazes run down a vertical surface.

I prepared another bowl in the same manner, but this time made the concentric circles using a combination of matte and gloss glazes. Over these I then applied the same five gloss glazes as in the pre-vious example. This produced some interesting effects, with the glazes running into one another.

APPLICATION TECHNIQUES

AS MENTIONED ABOVE, brushing colored glazes onto bisqueware is different from the way you apply underglazes. First, the consistency of a colored glaze should be about like heavy cream. Second, the application should be as even as possible, without leaving obvious brush marks or drips. In general, for consistent coverage, you must apply three even coats, letting each dry before applying the next one. (Note: Unlike clear glazes, commercial colored glazes don't usually come in a dipping formula.)

Beyond that basic advice, in this section I'll show you very briefly a few different techniques you can try with any combination of glazes. These involve layering, wax resist, masking, and just a bit more to whet your appetite for further exploration.

BOWL, DIAMETER 8" (20.3 CM). Here I simply layered one colored glaze over another; the combination produced a dramatic runny effect.

JOAN ROTHCHILD HARDIN, *BATIK APPLES,* 6 × 12" (15.2 × 30.5 CM). To create the two tiles in this composition, the artist began with a base colored glaze and painted other colored glazes over it.

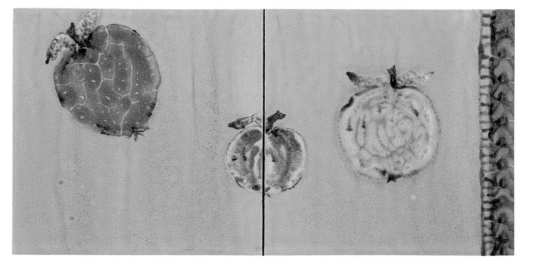

This technique involves using wax resist (the same kind you use on the bottom of a piece when clear glazing) to create a design. Apply two coats of a base colored glaze to your piece and let it dry completely. Then draw your design onto the piece with light pencil—or not, as you wish—then brush on a coat of wax resist in the desired pattern. (The wax will burn out in the kiln.) Let the wax resist dry completely. Make sure not to get wax resist on any part of the piece where you want the second layer of glaze. Carefully apply the second glaze over the first, brushing around the waxed areas, in two coats. When this is dry you can turn the piece over and glaze the bottom in a coordinating or contrasting glaze. As you see here, the color of the raw glaze (in this case brick red) does not correspond with its fired color (dull greenish brown).

Demonstration: WAX RESIST

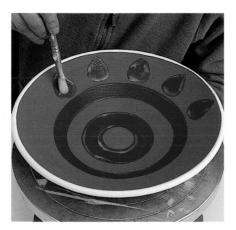

1 After applying two coats of my base color and letting it dry completely, I apply wax resist in my desired pattern.

2 When the wax resist is dry, I apply my second glaze color over the first in two coats, carefully brushing around the waxed areas.

3 The fired piece. Note how after firing, the brick-red raw glaze has become a dull greenish brown.

BOWL, DIAMETER 9" (22.9 CM).
I created the design on this bowl using the same wax-resist glaze-layering technique described in the demonstration.

Masking and Wax Resist

This is a technique to use when you want two (or more) glazes next to each other without their overlapping. It's a time-consuming approach, but it can produce stunning results, especially if the glazes are highly contrasting. Here I'm using a matte black glaze and a high-gloss amber glaze. As a masking material I'm using adhesive-backed paper.

Demonstration: COMBINING MASKING AND WAX RESIST

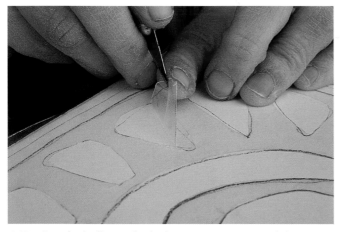

1 First I applied adhesive-backed paper to my piece and drew my design on it. (Alternatively, you can apply your design in separate cut-out shapes of adhesive paper, which may be easier on a curved surface.) Here I'm cutting out the design with a craft knife. Next, I smoothed down the adhesive paper to make sure it was secure.

2 I applied my first glaze, in three even coats, to the exposed areas and let it dry completely. I now apply a coat of wax resist over the glaze.

3 When the wax was dry I peeled up the adhesive paper, removing crumbs of dried glaze and wax from the surface with a soft brush. Now I apply my second glaze color, carefully working around the waxed areas; I use three coats. Once dry, the piece is ready to fire.

RIGHT: The fired tile. The contrast between the two colors and surfaces (matte and glossy) gives this piece a bold graphic quality.

Stained Glass Technique

This is another approach to use when you want to have glazes adjacent to one another without their overlapping. In this case there's a black line separating the glazes, resembling the leading in stained glass. The black line is created with a pigmented wax resist, applied with a brush or squeeze bottle. (During firing the wax melts but the pigment remains.) Various products are available for this purpose; here I used Waxline, from Axner Ceramic Supply (see "Sources" in the appendices). Alternatively, you can use your regular wax resist and then apply black ink, shoe polish, or paint to the unglazed lines after the piece has been fired. Note: Because the waxed line is unglazed, this technique is not appropriate for use on dinnerware or surfaces that come into contact with food.

For the demonstration shown below, I drew my quilt-block-style design in pencil directly on the bisque surface of an eight-inch-square tile, then applied the pigmented wax resist over the pencil lines with a fine brush. When the wax was dry, I applied glazes in the distinct areas created by the waxed lines. You can either brush the glaze on in three even coats, or let it flow from the brush in a thick layer, as I'm doing here The waxed lines repel the glaze, keeping each color within its enclosed area.

IRIS TRAY, 14 × 16" (35.6 × 40.6 CM). I decorated this tray using the stained glass technique.

Demonstration: STAINED GLASS TECHNIQUE

ABOVE: I let the glaze flow from my brush in a single, thick layer.

RIGHT: The fired piece. I used a clear crackle glaze as part of the design; to emphasize the crackle effect I rubbed India ink into the fine cracks.

Transparent Colored Glazes

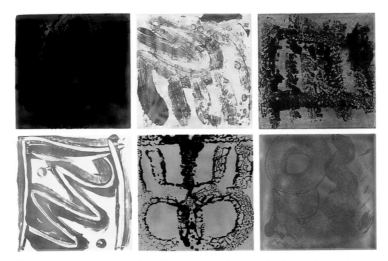

Fired results of tiles to which I first applied black underglaze using various transfer techniques, as described in chapter 3, then coated with some transparent and semitransparent colored glazes. Note the variety of effects.

Transparent colored glazes can be used with both underglazes and colored glazes for some interesting effects. The illustration at left shows you the fired results of my applications of transparent and semitransparent colored glazes over the black underglaze decoration on six tiles from the acetate and wax-paper transfer demonstrations in chapter 3. As you can see, the color of the glaze affects the color of the underglaze to varying degrees. In the turquoise tile, for example, the black underglaze looks blue. The illustration below left shows you the results I obtained by testing many transparent colored glazes over a spectrum of underglazes; in so doing I found that most seemed to obscure the underglaze colors. Note: Underglazes should be dry to the touch before you apply transparent colored glazes over them.

Another approach is to use a variety of colored glazes to decorate a bisque piece with patterns or motifs in the same way you'd do with underglazes. After that, you apply two or three even coats of a transparent colored glaze over the decorated surface. In the example shown on the opposite page at top left I used a transparent turquoise glaze over various matte colored glazes applied using brushing, stenciling, stamping, and trailing techniques, as demonstrated in chapter 3. You can do this in reverse as well (as exemplified by the pieces by Joan Rothchild Hardin, opposite): Apply a base colored glaze, then decorate over it. Refer to your glaze layering tests to determine which to use and in which order to layer them.

Here are my results from layering several transparent colored glazes over a spectrum of underglazes; note how the colored glazes seem to obscure the underglaze colors. Some results you'll get from doing these kinds of tests will be interesting, while others won't.

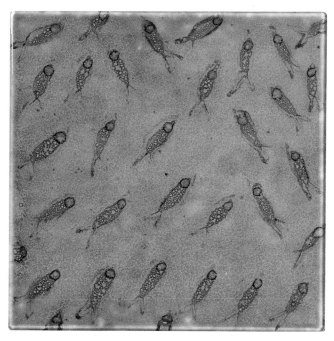

PLATTER, 11" (27.9 cm) SQUARE.

In this example I used a transparent turquoise glaze over various matte colored glazes applied using brushing, stenciling, stamping, and trailing techniques, as described in chapter 3.

JOAN ROTHCHILD HARDIN, *LITTLE FISH ON BLUE,* **8" (20.3 cm) SQUARE.**

This tile was created in the opposite manner; the artist applied a base colored glaze, then decorated over it.

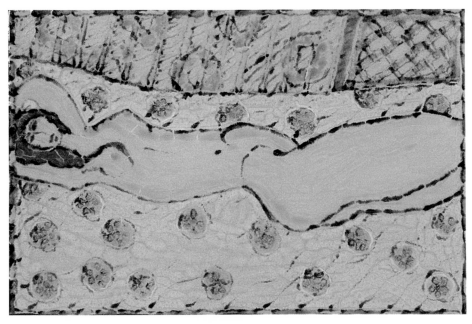

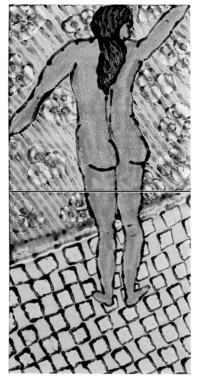

ABOVE: **JOAN ROTHCHILD HARDIN,** *WOMAN ON BED,* **8 × 12" (20.3 × 30.5 cm).**
RIGHT: **JOAN ROTHCHILD HARDIN,** *NUDE ON TILE FLOOR,* **12 × 6" (30.5 × 15.2 cm).**

These two pieces were made using colored glazes applied in a painterly way over a base colored glaze. At right, the artist composed her painting using two six-inch-square tiles as her "canvas."

Colored Glazes as Underglazes

I created the decorative lines on this vertical piece by applying colored glazes over the underglazes with a squeeze bottle, then clear-glazed and fired it; note how the colored glazes softened and began to run.

BELOW: **GARLIC BOWL, DIAMETER 13" (33 CM).**
The detail of my garlic bowl (below right) shows you how, thanks to gravity, the colored glaze dots of purple run a little bit downward on the vertical surface.

You can use colored glazes along with underglazes to create designs on bisqueware, coating the whole piece in the end with clear glaze before firing. Be aware that colored glazes used in this way are likely to run on a vertical surface. The purple dots on the garlic bowl shown below were made with a satin matte purple glaze; note that toward the bowl's rim these dots look as if they're about to drip downward. The decorative lines on the vertical piece in the illustration at left were created using colored glazes applied over the underglazes with a squeeze bottle before the piece was clear-glazed and fired; as with the dot motif on the garlic bowl, you can see how the colored glazes softened and began to run.

**HYDRANGEA PITCHER,
HEIGHT 8" (20.3 CM).**
Using an open-textured sponge,
I applied three different values
of blue colored glazes to define
the hydrangea blossoms.

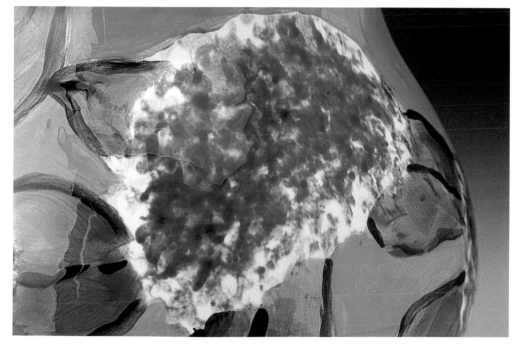

In this detail of the hydrangea
pitcher note how the glazes
appear soft and translucent.

POSTFIRING APPLICATIONS

WALL PIECE WITH LILIES, 28 × 10"
(71.1 × 25.4 CM).
To create this piece I used a combination of underglazes, clear glaze, colored glazes, and paper collage.

IN THIS SECTION I show you just a couple of methods for creating purely decorative bisqueware pieces—that is, wares not intended for food service. Glazes that result in dry matte or textured surfaces or crackled effects, or that contain lead or other toxic chemicals inappropriate for dinnerware, can be used on an array of other household objects such as lamps, clocks, decorative platters, and vases. Items like these can also incorporate nonceramic materials such as acrylic paint and paper collage, which offer a vast array of colors, textures, patterns, and surface qualities not easily achieved otherwise.

Though you can simply paint or collage a bisque piece and never fire it, I find it more interesting and challenging to integrate fired surfaces with nonfired surfaces, as the examples at left and on the opposite page illustrate.

To decorate a piece that integrates fired and nonfired surfaces, you have to plan ahead. First, in pencil, create the overall design on the piece. Next, decide which parts of your design are to be glazed (whether you're painting with underglazes and clear-glazing afterward, or using colored glazes), and which parts are to be left unglazed for postfiring applications. At this point you should have an idea as to how you will treat these unglazed portions, but you need not make final decisions in terms of materials and techniques. After you've glazed and fired your piece, you can treat the unglazed parts with paint, collage, gold leaf, or whatever nonceramic material you choose.

Various papers and acrylic paints that can be used in postfiring decorating techniques.

LAMP WITH HANDPAINTED SHADE, HEIGHT 19" (48.3 CM).
I treated this lamp base with high-gloss black and amber glazes and, after firing, applied screen-printed paper and green and gold acrylics to it. I painted the lampshade in acrylics, using a decorative-paper edging along the bottom.

VASE, HEIGHT 13" (33 CM); SLAB-BUILT WITH GLAZED AND COLLAGE DECORATION.
Here I used underglazes, clear glaze, and paper collage. I dyed some highly textural papers with watercolor dyes before cutting out and applying the shapes to the piece.

Collage and Acrylics

To decorate the platter in the demonstration below, I divided the surface into uneven quadrants with a pencil, then drew patterns on each of those sections that overlapped the lines of the composition. I applied wax resist to the portions I wanted to leave unglazed for postfiring treatment, then used a variety of colored glazes and underglazes to fill in the patterns. After firing, I used decorative papers and acrylic paint to complete the piece.

All of the underglaze techniques discussed in chapter 3 are applicable to the use of acrylic paint. (Note: There are many books available on decorative painting techniques, which you may find useful if you want to explore further.) As for collage techniques, here I show you one that's specific to postfiring decoration: applying paper collage to unglazed areas within glazed areas or those surrounding them.

Demonstration: COLLAGE AND ACRYLICS

1 The fired platter before collage and acrylic applications.

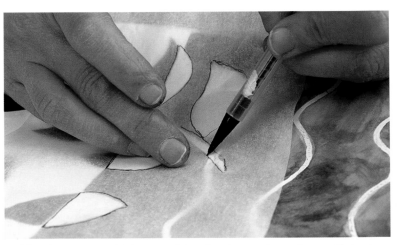

2 After determining which parts of the piece I wanted to collage, with tracing paper I traced around those areas with a soft pencil.

3 Next, I placed the traced pencil-drawn design(s) face down on my decorative paper and transferred them to that surface by going over the lines with a ballpoint pen.

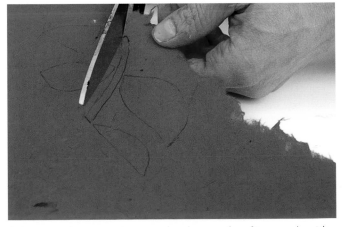

4 I cut out the paper shapes and make sure they fit properly with my intended design.

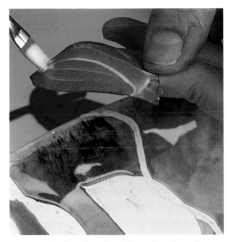  

5 I apply glue (preferably archival quality PVA) to the reverse sides of these shapes . . .

6 . . . and stick them onto the bisque form.

7 Now I cover all of my collage appliqués with a coat of clear matte acrylic medium.

PLATTER, DIAMETER 16" (40.6 CM).
Here's the finished version of the decorative platter I made for this demonstration.

enter the cone number to which you wish to fire, and the speed— fast, medium, or slow. You can usually program the controller to hold the temperature for a given period, an approach called "soaking," which helps glazes to mature fully. In the "ramp/hold" mode you program rates of temperature increase (and decrease if you want a slow cooling cycle) in segments. The "hold" feature allows you to maintain the temperature at the end of any segment, which gives you a great deal of flexibility to experiment with different firing cycles, an especially interesting option in the use of colored glazes and specialty glazes.

The price difference between manual and automatic versions of the same kiln model can be several hundred dollars, but the freedom you gain from having an automatic temperature controller may be well worth it. However, if you opt for a manual kiln, it can be upgraded to an automatic with an external temperature controller.

Here's a typical way a kiln might be loaded. At bottom are four short kiln posts supporting the first shelf layer. The next four posts sit directly above the preceding ones and are proportionate in height to the wares on that level. On the shelf above, note the short post between the two mugs; atop it is a horizontally placed pyrometric cone, which helps gauge firing temperature. The cone is viewed through a spy hole on the outside of the kiln.

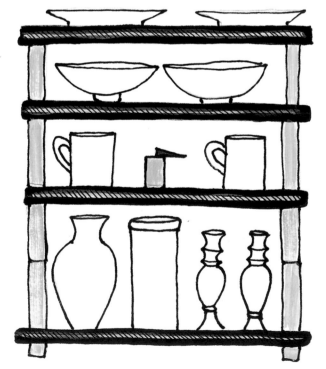

ELECTRICAL SERVICE

No matter what type of electrical service you have, you can get a kiln that will work for you. Have an electrician check your voltage and amperage to ensure that your kiln is equipped with the appropriate wiring and heating elements and that operating the kiln will not conflict with your other appliances. In any case, all the electrical information you need to know is provided in the manufacturer's product specifications, and is also printed on a tag on the kiln itself for easy reference.

FIREBRICK THICKNESS

Most kiln manufacturers offer various options as to basic structural components and overall quality, reflected, of course, in price. One involves the firebricks that make up the main structure of the kiln; these are either 2½" or 3" (6.4 or 7.6 cm) thick. For ceramics the 3" thickness is much

better, as its insulating capacity allows your kiln not only to heat efficiently, but also to cool slowly once it is shut off, which can make a difference in your glaze results.

KILN ACCESSORIES

Once you've chosen the right kiln for your needs, you'll have to purchase a few other items for it. The major expense here is kiln furniture, which consists of kiln shelves and the posts that hold them up. Shelves are costly (expect to pay several hundred dollars for those for a medium-size kiln), but they last forever. Posts are cheap, and I recommend getting a variety of sizes. You want short ones for shelves on which you place tiles or plates, medium ones for mugs and bowls, tall ones for vases and pitchers, and so forth. You'll also need posts on which to set cones so you can see them through kiln peepholes.

Some kiln manufacturers offer a packaged set of furniture for each kiln, but you can also buy shelves and posts individually. If you're primarily making tiles or plates, you'll need more shelves and shorter posts; if you're making mostly tall pieces, you'll need fewer shelves and taller posts.

To care for kiln shelves, scrape them down with a metal putty knife or paint scraper and apply fresh kiln wash every few firings. If glaze drips onto a kiln shelf, scrape it off right away and apply fresh kiln wash to the affected area.

Another kiln accessory to consider is a venting system. It's a good idea— although not absolutely essential— to vent your kiln, especially if it's in your residence. Kiln manufacturers usually offer such systems and can recommend the right one for your setup. Alternatively, you can make your own.

FIRING

BISQUEWARE, as used in all the techniques throughout this book, has been fired once, or "bisque fired," meaning that all the significant changes from raw clay to fired ceramics have taken place. Glaze firing—the second firing done after wares have been glazed—primarily concerns the changes that take place in the glaze. During the firing, a glaze melts into a liquid state and its raw ingredients fuse into a molten glass. As the kiln cools, the glaze again becomes solid, but its character has been completely altered from that of its raw state.

During the first part of the firing, up to about 250° F, you increase the kiln temperature slowly, so as not to subject the wares to thermal shock. Also, there is still some water in the glaze, which should evaporate slowly. A safe rate of temperature increase for this segment is 150° F per hour. Between 250° F and 1700° F you can raise the temperature more quickly, at around 250° F per hour. For the last phase of the firing, the last two hundred degrees or so, you slow the heating rate to about 125° F per hour. This helps to even out the kiln temperature and allows the glazes to mature fully.

How long does the firing process take? This depends on two main factors, the first being the size of your kiln. Bigger kilns take longer to heat up and cool down than do smaller ones. The second factor is thermal density, or the mass of stuff in your kiln. A more densely loaded kiln will require more time to complete the firing cycle than a sparsely loaded kiln, even if you program it for the same firing schedule. Kiln shelves have more mass than bisqueware, so that the number of shelves in the kiln has a bigger effect on firing time than the quantity of wares. I routinely program my ten-cubic-foot kiln to fire at a medium speed to cone 05. This can take anywhere from seven and a half hours to almost nine hours.

Pyrometric cones are used to monitor firings and determine when a firing is finished. Why do we use cones rather than temperature readings given in degrees? Because heat absorption is the factor that determines when your glazes have melted and fused properly. Cones are composed of ceramic materials determined to soften, and eventually melt, when a given amount of heat has been absorbed. Each cone number indicates a different amount of heat absorption required for the cone to soften, or bend. The higher the number, the more heat the cone must absorb. A zero (0) preceding a cone number functions like the minus sign in a negative number, such that cone 04 is hotter than cone 05.

Heat absorption depends on both time and temperature. The faster the firing, the higher the temperature it is necessary to reach for a given amount of heat to be absorbed. The slower the firing, the lower the temperature it is necessary to reach for the same amount of heat to be absorbed. For example, a firing done at a rate of 270° F per hour will have to reach 1911° F for cone 05 to bend, while a firing done at a rate of 108° F per hour will have to reach 1888° F for cone 05 to bend. If you "soak" your kiln—that is, hold it at its final temperature before letting it cool—ceramic changes will continue to take place. A one- to two-hour soak is enough for the next higher numbered cone to bend. If you were to determine when your firing was done by temperature alone, you could easily shut off your kiln before the glazes had melted properly, or leave it on too long and have your glazes bubble and drip. We do speak of cone numbers as measuring kiln temperature, but "temperature" is used loosely, as we're really talking about heat absorption.

With an automatic kiln, cones are used either as a backup for your temperature controller, or to get temperature readings in different parts of the kiln. The automatic controller can measure the temperature only around where the thermocouple is located, usually near the middle of the kiln. To check how even the temperature is throughout the kiln, you may want to place cones on short posts in the upper and lower portions of the kiln as well. (The cone is placed on a separate post that sits on a kiln shelf between taller posts supporting the next shelf.) If your kiln is firing unevenly, it helps to slow down the firing cycle, especially during the last two hundred degrees, or soak it for fifteen to twenty minutes when it reaches temperature.

With a manual kiln, it's essential that you be able to see your cones. Whereas with an automatic kiln, using one cone (the one indicating the final kiln temperature) is sufficient, with a manual kiln it is best to use, in addition, one and two cones below your final temperature. This way you can see when your firing cycle is close to finished. (See the heading "Temperature Control" in the section on kilns.)

How do you know when the cone is bent enough to indicate that the kiln has reached its final temperature? If your cone is horizontal to start with, consider it bent when it is pointing to five o'clock. Once the cone starts to bend, it usually takes fifteen to twenty minutes for it to reach this position. The difference between the cone being bent at five o'clock and pointing straight down is negligible. If the cone has melted and fused to the kiln post, you have gone beyond its temperature indication.

For more information about pyrometric cones and firing, contact: The Edward Orton Jr. Ceramic Foundation, P.O. Box 2760, Westerville, OH 43086-2760, 614-895-2663, www.ortonceramic.com.

SOURCES

Here is a list of manufacturers and suppliers of materials used in decorating ceramics.

UNDERGLAZE AND GLAZE MANUFACTURERS

Following the various manufacturers' names and contact information, I've listed the products they offer (though by no means comprehensively) that are relevant to the contents of this book and further exploration of the medium. Contact individual manufacturers for complete product information and a list of distributors.

AMACO
American Art Clay Co., Inc.
Indianapolis, Indiana 46222
1-800-374-1600
www.amaco.com
Underglazes, glazes, majolica glaze with decorating colors, overglazes (metallics, lustres, china paints, not discussed in this book), tools and accessories, equipment, educational support.

Axner Company, Inc.
490 Kane Court
P.O. Box 621484
Oviedo, Florida 32765
1-800-843-7057
Axner is primarily a distributor for other manufacturers' products. However, the company does produce its own underglaze pens, wax resist, kiln wash, kilns, and several other products. They carry Waxline, discussed in chapter 4.

Duncan Enterprises
5673 East Shields Avenue
Fresno, California 93727
1-800-CERAMIC (237-2642)
www.duncanceramics.com
Underglazes, glazes, wax resist, specialty products, overglazes (metallics and lustres, not discussed), acrylic products and accessories, brushes, decorating tools, instructional literature.

Gare, Inc.
165 Rosemont Street
Haverill, Massachusetts 01830
978-373-9131
www.gare.com
Underglazes, glazes, overglaze metallics (not discussed), tools and accessories, equipment, instructional information, acrylic products and accessories.

Mayco
4077 Weaver Court South
Hilliard, Ohio 43026
614-876-1171
www.maycocolors.com
info@maycocolors.com
Underglazes, glazes, specialty products, acrylic products and accessories, brushes, tools, overglazes (metallics and lustres, not discussed). For technical service: technical@maycocolors.com or 614-675-2031.

Spectrum Glazes, Inc.
40 Hanlan Road,
    Units 32 and 33
Woodbridge, Ontario,
    Canada L4L 3P6
and P.O. Box 874
Lewiston, New York 14092
1-800-970-1970
Underglazes, glazes, majolica glaze with decorating colors, and specialty products.

BISQUEWARE

Aftosa Bisque
1034 Ohio Avenue
Richmond, California 94804
1-800-231-0397
www.aftosa.com

Bella Bisque, Inc.
P.O. Box 1212
Kyle, Texas 78640
1-800-90-BELLA
www.bellabisque.com

Bisque Imports
53 Ervin Street
Belmont, North Carolina
    28012
1-888-568-5991
www.bisqueimports.com

Ceramica Imports
928 Broadway, Suite 1101
New York, NY 10010
1-888-4BISK-33
www.ceramicaimports.com

Ceramic Supply of New York
    and New Jersey
7 Route 46 West
Lodi, New Jersey 07644
1-800-7CERAMIC
www.7ceramic.com

Chesapeake Ceramic Supply
4706 Benson Avenue
Baltimore, Maryland 21227
1-800-962-9655
www.ceramicsupply.com

Gare/Bisquefire
165 Rosemont Street
Haverill, Massachusetts 01830
1-888-289-4273
www.gare.com

Pull Cart, Inc.
P.O. Box 181
Montclair, New Jersey 07042
1-888-PULCART
www.pullcartbisque.com

TILES

Many of the bisqueware suppliers also carry tiles, but for a unique variety, accessories, and volume discounts, I recommend:

Manitou Arts
P.O. Box 910
Leland, Michigan 49654
1-866-240-3434
www.manitouarts.com

KILNS

Cress Mfg. Company:
    www.cressmfg.com
Gare Kilns (made by Evenheat):
    www.evenheat-kiln.com
L & L Kiln Mfg.:
    www.hotkilns.com
Olympic Kilns:
    kilns-kilns.com
Paragon Industries:
    www.paragonweb.com
Skutt Ceramic Products:
    www.skutt.com

CONTEMPORARY STUDIOS

For your nearest contemporary ceramics studio, check your local yellow pages or the Web site of the Contemporary Ceramic Studios Association (CCSA): www.ccsaonline.com

CONTRIBUTORS

GEORGANNA GAY, known as Janno, received her BFA in glass sculpture in 1985 from the California College of Arts and Crafts, Oakland. Subsequently she moved to Vermont and turned to pottery making, discovering that the beautifully white surface of low-fire earthenware was conducive to creating pictures on pots in a way that allowed her to combine art with function. She uses her own majolica recipe to decorate her pottery, choosing images from the natural world such as birds, flowers, fruit, vegetables, and fish. Gay maintains a studio and gallery in Dorset, Vermont. Contact information:
Flower Brook Pottery
P.O. Box 472–Route 30
Corner of Dorset Hollow Road
Dorset, VT 05251
Telephone: 802-867-2409
www.flowerbrookpottery.com

JOAN ROTHCHILD HARDIN has been a ceramic artist since 1969 and today specializes in handpainted art tiles for installation as murals, friezes, and other applications. Her tile designs have been commissioned for residential, corporate, and commercial settings across the country, including projects for three veterinary hospitals in New York City and company logo tiles for Al Benessere, a line of aromatherapy products. Hardin's subject matter includes abstracts, flowers, still lifes, animals, women, Judaica, house numbers, and more. Her award-winning work has been shown in museums and galleries; is in private and corporate collections in the U.S.,

Australia, and Europe; and is represented in the slide registries of the Tile Heritage Foundation and New York City's Percent for Art Program. Her tiles have been featured in such publications as *Ceramic Art Tile for the Home* (Schiffer, 2001); several sourcebooks published by The Guild; and *Ceramics Monthly* and *Pottery Making Illustrated.*

Hardin is a co-owner of Brooklyn Artisans Gallery, a fine crafts gallery in Cobble Hill, Brooklyn. She has also been a ceramics teacher and an art-show judge and has been listed in *Who's Who in the East* and *Who's Who of American Women.* Contact information:
393 West Broadway, #4
New York, NY 10012
Telephone: 212-966-9433
Fax: 212-431-9196
www.hardintiles.com

SUSAN KRAMER received a BA in studio art from the University of Vermont and later earned an MS degree in art education from Central Connecticut State University. She has been smitten with the clay bug since 1986 and has been in business as a solo artisan since 1997. Her work can be found at fine crafts shows in southern Vermont and at a few select galleries in the Northeast.

Kramer professes an affinity for abstract painting, citing the large color blocks of Mark Rothko and Hans Hofmann and the bold black brushstrokes of Robert Motherwell as particular inspirations. She discovered the expressive qualities of clay while spending time in Japan as an exchange student, and

today combines her chosen medium with her love of abstract expressionism, using clay as a canvas upon which to paint her colorscapes.

KRISTEN MILLS studied at Massachusetts College of Art in Boston, then earned her BFA in visual communications at Rivier College in Nashua, New Hampshire, in 1996. Shortly thereafter she became a certified teacher of K-12 art and taught at the Nashua Child Learning Center. She relocated to Boston in 1998 to make her mark on the art scene there.

After a stint as a scenic painter, Mills contracted her own mural work with such clients as Iris Associates and Lotus Development Corporation. She freelances as an illustrator of children's educational science kits for XLibris in Hamilton, Massachusetts, and also assists Jane Davies with her ceramics.

Mills's work has been exhibited in various Boston-area settings, including the United South End Open Studios, 29 Newbury Street, the Landau Gallery, and Zeitgeist Gallery. At this latter venue, in Cambridge, she began collaborating with musicians by painting and drawing to live jazz, and now maintains a monthly gig there creating work in front of an audience.

With a fluid gestural style, bold colors, and confident brushstrokes that manifest her love of drawing and painting, Mills creates a mood through strong contrasts of lights and darks and an intuitive sense of composition. She maintains a

painting studio in Hyde Park, Massachusetts.
www.kmillsstudios.com

JOHN POLAK has been a professional photographer since 1978, beginning with assignments for commercial clients and then moving on to the art world, where he specializes in photographing works by crafts artists and fine artists. Polak has worked for the Springfield Museum of Fine Arts and the George Walter Vincent Smith Art Museum, both in western Massachusetts. He is also a founding member of Zone Art Center, an artist-run facility in Springfield. His photos have been featured in such publications as *Ceramics Monthly, American Craft, The Crafts Report,* and *Art New England.* Polak is based in Chicopee, Massachusetts; he can be reached at his studio by telephone at 800-474-6865.

SUSAN STEINBERG is founder of Steinberg Designs LLC, in Sherman, Connecticut. With more than a decade of experience in the field of surface design, she sells and licenses her work to many leading companies. Steinberg is an expert at solving clients' design dilemmas. Brainstorming with staff to create fresh new looks in tabletop and gift products, she brings their visions to fruition. Among her clients are Bennington Pottery, Dansk, Deruta, Georgia Pacific, Mikasa, and Pfaltzgraff, to name just a few. Steinberg's stated goal is to contribute joy and satisfaction to people through her designs.

INDEX